how to get your
five-a-day
the fruit and vegetable cookbook

how to get your

five-a-day

the fruit and vegetable cookbook

over 50 delicious step-by-step recipes
for health and long life

christine ingram and maggie mayhew

southwater

This edition is published by Southwater

Southwater is an imprint of Anness Publishing Ltd
Hermes House, 88–89 Blackfriars Road, London SE1 8HA
tel. 020 7401 2077; fax 020 7633 9499
www.southwaterbooks.com; info@anness.com

© Anness Publishing Ltd 2005

UK agent: The Manning Partnership Ltd
6 The Old Dairy, Melcombe Road, Bath BA2 3LR
tel. 01225 478444; fax 01225 478440
sales@manning-partnership.co.uk

UK distributor: Grantham Book Services Ltd
Isaac Newton Way, Alma Park Industrial Estate
Grantham, Lincs NG31 9SD
tel. 01476 541080; fax 01476 541061
orders@gbs.tbs-ltd.co.uk

North American agent/distributor: National Book Network
4501 Forbes Boulevard, Suite 200, Lanham, MD 20706
tel. 301 459 3366; fax 301 429 5746
www.nbnbooks.com

Australian agent/distributor: Pan Macmillan Australia
Level 18, St Martins Tower, 31 Market St, Sydney, NSW 2000
tel. 1300 135 113; fax 1300 135 103
customer.service@macmillan.com.au

New Zealand agent/distributor: David Bateman Ltd
30 Tarndale Grove, Off Bush Road, Albany, Auckland
tel. (09) 415 7664; fax (09) 415 8892

A CIP catalogue record for this book is available from the
British Library.

Publisher: Joanna Lorenz
Editorial Director: Helen Sudell
Editors: Linda Fraser and Elizabeth Woodland
Designers: Nigel Partridge and Patrick McLeavey
Jacket Designer: Whitelight Design Associates
Photography and styling: William Lingwood (fruit recipes)
and Patrick McLeavey (vegetable recipes)
Food for photography: Bridget Sargeson (fruit recipes),
Christine France (fruits) and Jane Stevenson (vegetables)
Indexer: Hilary Bird
Production Controller: Darren Price

Previously published as part of a larger volume, *Five-a-Day
Fruit & Vegetable Cookbook*

10 9 8 7 6 5 4 3 2 1

NOTES

Bracketed terms are intended for American readers. For all
recipes, quantities are given in both metric and imperial
measures and, where appropriate, measures are also given in
standard cups and spoons. Follow one set, but not a mixture,
because they are not interchangeable.

Standard spoon and cup measures are level.
1 tsp = 5ml, 1 tbsp = 15ml, 1 cup = 250ml/8fl oz

Australian standard tablespoons are 20ml. Australian readers
should use 3 tsp in place of 1 tbsp for measuring small
quantities of gelatine, flour, salt etc.

Medium (US large) eggs are used unless otherwise stated.

The diets and information in this book are not intended to
replace advice from a qualified medical practitioner, doctor
or dietician. Always consult your health practitioner before
adopting any of the suggestions in this book. Neither the
authors nor the publishers can accept any liability for failure
to follow this advice.

CONTENTS

MAKE IT FIVE

Research has shown that eating a balanced diet with at least five portions of fruit and vegetables a day can significantly reduce the risk of many chronic diseases such as heart disease, cancer and stroke as well as offering many other health benefits. Eating more of them can also help you to increase fibre intake, reduce fat intake and maintain a healthy weight.

Frozen fruit and vegetables are just as good as fresh, and are sometimes even better because they are frozen so soon after picking. Canned fruit and vegetables make a good substitute, but try to buy ones canned in water or fruit juice rather than brine or sugar syrup.

Balance and Variety

Eating a healthy diet doesn't have to mean giving up all your favourite foods. It's all about balance and making sure you eat the right proportions of the right foods. Balance, moderation and variety are the key words.

There are five main food groups: starchy foods such as potatoes, pasta and bread; fruit and vegetables; dairy foods such as milk, yogurt and cheese; protein foods such as meat, chicken, fish and tofu; and foods high in fat and sugar such as cakes and cookies.

Starchy foods and fruit and vegetables should make up the largest part of each meal. Protein foods and dairy products are important, but should be eaten in moderation. Fatty and sugary foods should be enjoyed only as an occasional treat.

As with all foods, different types of fruit and vegetables contain different combinations of fibre and nutrients. To ensure you obtain the maximum benefit, make sure you eat a variety.

How Big is a Portion?

The size of a portion, and how many times you can count it in a single day, varies depending on the type of fruit or vegetable. Use the table below to check whether you're eating enough.

ONE PORTION	HOW MUCH IS THAT?	HOW DOES IT COUNT?
Fruit (fresh, frozen or canned)	• 1 medium-size piece of fruit such as an apple or banana • 2 smaller pieces of fruit such as satsumas or figs • a handful of small fruits such as grapes or strawberries • 3 heaped tablespoons of fruit salad • half a larger piece of fruit such as a grapefruit • 5cm/2in slice of very large fruit such as melon	Every portion of fruit you eat counts towards your daily five.
Dried fruit	• 3 small fruits such as apricots • 15ml/1 tbsp very small dried fruits such as raisins	Dried fruit counts as only one portion a day, no matter how much of it you eat.
100% pure fruit or vegetable juice	• one glass	Juices count as only one portion a day, no matter how many glasses of juice you drink.
Vegetables	• 3 heaped tablespoons cooked vegetables such as carrots or peas	Every portion of vegetables you eat counts towards your daily five. **But remember** – potatoes are counted as a starchy food, not a vegetable, so they can't be included in your daily five portions.
Salad	• 1 cereal bowl	Every portion of salad you eat counts towards your daily five.
Beans and lentils	• 45ml/3 tbsp cooked beans or lentils such as kidney beans or chickpeas	Beans and lentils count as only one portion a day, no matter how many portions you eat.

Easy Ways to Five

If you don't usually eat five portions of fruit and vegetables a day, achieving this target can sometimes seem like an unmanageable task. The good news is that it doesn't need to be a struggle. There are so many delicious ways to prepare fruit and vegetables, and clever ways to "sneak" them into your diet, that you'll find it a pure pleasure achieving your daily target. Listed below are some simple ways to work more fruits and vegetables into your diet.

• Enjoy a fresh fruit smoothie at any time of day. Simply blend soft fruits such as raspberries or mangoes with milk to make a rich, creamy drink that is packed with nutrients. Unlike fruit juices, smoothies still contain all the fibre of the original fruit.
• Add a chopped banana, or a handful of strawberries or raisins to a bowl of cereal in the morning. It will taste like a special breakfast but it's actually helping you on your way to five-a-day.
• When you feel like a sweet treat, eat a few dried apricots or figs instead of reaching for the cookie tin. They taste just as sweet, but they're healthier and can count as one of your portions.

Above: Snacking on raw vegetables is an easy way to eat more fruit and veg. They taste great and are low in fat too.

• Instead of spreading jam on your toast, use a mashed banana. It tastes great and is so much healthier than a sugar-packed spread.
• Desserts and cakes don't need to be all bad. Although they are high in fat and sugar so should be eaten in moderation, choosing a slice of cake packed with dried fruit, or a dessert

Above: Drink your way to five portions a day with a delicious, healthy blend of ripe strawberries, yogurt and milk.

containing lots of fruit will contribute to your five daily portions – rather than just offering empty calories.
• When making sandwiches, add plenty of extra salad. They will look more appealing and taste much nicer.
• Chopped raw vegetables such as carrots, cucumber and (bell) peppers make a great snack at any time of day and are so much healthier than a packet of potato crisps (chips) or a cookie.
• Add a few extra chopped vegetables to non-vegetable dishes such as meat stews, or stir baby spinach into mashed potatoes just before serving.

About this Book

The recipes in this book have been specially designed to make the most of the delicious fruits and vegetables that are available in the supermarket, helping you to enjoy a tastier, healthier diet. There is a huge choice of recipes for every occasion – from healthy salads and low-fat desserts, to rich and creamy risottos, spicy curries, golden pies and pizzas and indulgent cakes. No matter what your mood, you are sure to find the perfect recipe to help you on your way to five-a-day.

Left: Eating a variety of different fruits and vegetables every day is essential to good health.

ROOTS, SHOOTS AND STEMS

For tasty, nourishing meals, you don't need to look further than roots, shoots and stems, whether it is carrots, parsnips, asparagus or onions. Yam Fritters or Carrot and Coriander Soup are the stuff of winter evenings — warm and filling, simple to make, great to eat.

CARROT AND CORIANDER SOUP

NEARLY ALL ROOT VEGETABLES MAKE EXCELLENT SOUPS AS THEY PURÉE WELL AND HAVE AN EARTHY FLAVOUR WHICH COMPLEMENTS THE SHARPER FLAVOURS OF HERBS AND SPICES. CARROTS ARE PARTICULARLY VERSATILE AND THIS SIMPLE SOUP IS ELEGANT IN BOTH FLAVOUR AND APPEARANCE.

SERVES FOUR TO SIX

INGREDIENTS

450g/1lb carrots, preferably young
   and tender
15ml/1 tbsp sunflower oil
40g/1½oz/3 tbsp butter
1 onion, chopped
1 celery stalk, sliced plus 2–3 pale
   leafy celery tops
2 small potatoes, chopped
1 litre/1¾ pints/4 cups chicken stock
10–15ml/2–3 tsp ground coriander
15ml/1 tbsp chopped fresh coriander
   (cilantro)
200ml/7fl oz/⅞ cup milk
salt and freshly ground black pepper

1 Trim the carrots, peel if necessary and cut into chunks. Heat the oil and 25g/1oz/2 tbsp of the butter in a large flameproof casserole or heavy pan and fry the onion over a gentle heat for 3–4 minutes until they are slightly softened but not browned.

2 Cut the celery stalk into slices. Add the celery and potatoes to the onion in the pan, cook for a few minutes and then add the carrots. Fry over a gentle heat for 3–4 minutes, stirring frequently, and then cover. Reduce the heat even further and sweat for about 10 minutes. Shake the pan or stir occasionally so the vegetables do not stick to the base.

3 Add the stock, bring to the boil and then partially cover and simmer for a further 8–10 minutes until the carrots and potatoes are tender.

4 Remove 6–8 tiny celery leaves for garnish and finely chop the remaining celery tops (about 15ml/1 tbsp once chopped). Melt the remaining butter in a small pan and fry the ground coriander for about 1 minute, stirring all the time.

5 Reduce the heat and then add the chopped celery and fresh coriander and fry for about 1 minute. Set aside.

6 Purée the soup in a food processor or blender and pour into a clean pan. Stir in the milk, coriander mixture and seasoning. Heat gently, taste and adjust the seasoning. Serve garnished with the reserved celery.

COOK'S TIP
For a more piquant flavour, add a little lemon juice just before serving.

PARSNIP AND CHESTNUT CROQUETTES

THE SWEET NUTTY TASTE OF CHESTNUTS BLENDS PERFECTLY WITH THE SIMILARLY SWEET BUT EARTHY FLAVOUR OF PARSNIPS. FRESH CHESTNUTS NEED TO BE PEELED BUT FROZEN CHESTNUTS ARE EASY TO USE AND ARE NEARLY AS GOOD AS FRESH FOR THIS RECIPE.

MAKES TEN TO TWELVE

INGREDIENTS

450g/1lb parsnips, cut roughly into
   small pieces
115g/4oz/1 cup frozen chestnuts
25g/1oz/2 tbsp butter
1 garlic clove, crushed
15ml/1 tbsp chopped fresh coriander
   (cilantro)
1 egg, beaten
40–50g/1½–2oz fresh white
   breadcrumbs
vegetable oil, for frying
salt and freshly ground black pepper
sprigs of coriander (cilantro), to garnish

1 Place the parsnips in a pan with enough water to cover. Bring to the boil, cover and simmer for 15–20 minutes until completely tender.

2 Place the frozen chestnuts in a pan of water, bring to the boil and simmer for 8–10 minutes until very tender. Drain, place in a bowl and mash roughly.

3 Melt the butter in a small pan and cook the garlic for 30 seconds. Drain the parsnips and mash with the garlic butter. Stir in the chestnuts and chopped coriander, then season well.

4 Take about 30–45ml/2–3 tbsp of the mixture at a time and form into small croquettes, about 7.5cm/3in long. Dip each one into the beaten egg and then roll in the fresh white breadcrumbs.

5 Heat a little oil in a frying pan and fry the croquettes for 3–4 minutes until golden, turning frequently so they brown evenly. Drain on kitchen paper and then serve at once, garnished with coriander.

FENNEL AND MUSSEL PROVENÇAL

SERVES FOUR

INGREDIENTS
2 large fennel bulbs
1.75kg/4–4½lb fresh mussels in
  their shells, well scrubbed under
  cold water and beards removed
175ml/6fl oz/¾ cup water
a sprig of thyme
25g/1oz/2 tbsp butter
4 shallots, finely chopped
1 garlic clove, crushed
250ml/8fl oz/1 cup white wine
10ml/2 tsp plain (all-purpose) flour
175ml/6fl oz/¾ cup single (light)
  cream
15ml/1 tbsp chopped fresh parsley
salt and freshly ground black pepper
a sprig of dill, to garnish

1 Trim the fennel, cut into slices
5mm/¼in thick and then cut into
1cm/½in sticks. Cook in a little salted
water until just tender, then drain.

2 Discard any mussels that are
damaged or do not close. Put in a large
pan, add the water and thyme, cover
tightly, bring to the boil and cook for
about 5 minutes until the mussels open,
shaking occasionally.

3 Transfer the mussels to a plate and
discard any that are unopened. When
cool enough to handle, remove them
from their shells, reserving a few in their
shells for the garnish.

4 Melt the butter in a pan and fry the
shallots and garlic for 3–4 minutes until
softened but not browned. Add the
fennel, fry briefly for 30–60 seconds and
then stir in the wine and simmer gently
until the liquid is reduced by half.

5 Blend the flour with a little extra wine
or water. Add the cream, parsley and
seasoning to the pan and heat gently.
Stir in the blended flour and the
mussels. Cook over a low heat until the
sauce thickens. Season and pour into a
warmed serving dish. Garnish with dill
and the reserved mussels in their shells.

BRAISED FENNEL WITH TOMATOES

SERVES FOUR

INGREDIENTS
3 small fennel bulbs
30–45ml/2–3 tbsp olive oil
5–6 shallots, sliced
2 garlic cloves, crushed
4 tomatoes, peeled and chopped
about 175ml/6fl oz/¾ cup dry
  white wine
15ml/1 tbsp chopped fresh basil or
  2.5ml/½ tsp dried
40–50g/1½–2oz/¾–1cup fresh white
  breadcrumbs
salt and freshly ground black pepper

1 Preheat the oven to 150°C/300°F/
Gas 2. Trim the fennel bulbs and cut into
slices about 1cm/½ in thick.

2 Heat the olive oil in a large pan and
fry the shallots and garlic for about 4–5
minutes over a moderate heat until the
shallots are slightly softened. Add the
tomatoes, stir-fry briefly and then stir in
150ml/¼ pint/⅔ cup of the wine, the basil
and seasoning. Bring to the boil, add the
fennel, then cover and cook for 5 minutes.

3 Arrange the fennel in layers in an
ovenproof dish. Pour over the tomato
mixture and sprinkle the top with half the
breadcrumbs. Bake in the oven for about
1 hour. From time to time, press down on
the breadcrumb crust with the back of a
spoon and sprinkle over another layer of
breadcrumbs and a little more of the
wine. The crust slowly becomes golden
brown and very crunchy.

YAM FRITTERS

YAMS HAVE A SLIGHTLY DRIER FLAVOUR THAN POTATOES AND ARE PARTICULARLY GOOD WHEN MIXED WITH SPICES AND THEN FRIED. THE FRITTERS CAN ALSO BE MOULDED INTO SMALL BALLS AND DEEP FRIED. THIS IS A FAVOURITE AFRICAN WAY OF SERVING YAMS.

MAKES ABOUT 18–20

INGREDIENTS
    675g/1½lb yams
    milk, for mashing
    2 small (US medium) eggs, beaten
    45ml/3 tbsp chopped tomato flesh
    45ml/3 tbsp finely chopped spring
        onions (scallions)
    1 green chilli, seeded and
        finely sliced
    flour, for shaping
    40g/1½oz/¾ cup white breadcrumbs
    vegetable oil, for shallow frying
    salt and freshly ground black pepper

1 Peel the yams and cut into chunks. Place in a pan of salted water and boil for 20–30 minutes until tender. Drain and mash with a little milk and about 45ml/3 tbsp of the beaten eggs.

2 Add the chopped tomato, spring onions, chilli and seasoning and stir well to mix thoroughly.

3 Using floured hands, shape the yam and vegetable mixture into round fritters, about 7.5cm/3in in diameter.

4 Dip each in the remaining egg and then coat evenly with the breadcrumbs. Heat a little oil in a large frying pan and fry the fritters for about 4–5 minutes until golden brown. Turn the fritters over once during cooking. Drain well on kitchen paper and serve.

TARO, CARROT AND PARSNIP MEDLEY

TARO, LIKE YAMS, IS WIDELY EATEN IN AFRICA AND THE CARIBBEAN, OFTEN AS A PURÉE. HERE, IT IS ROASTED AND COMBINED WITH MORE COMMON ROOT VEGETABLES TO MAKE A COLOURFUL DISPLAY.

SERVES FOUR TO SIX

INGREDIENTS
    450g/1lb taros
    350g/12oz parsnips
    450g/1lb carrots
    25g/1oz/2 tbsp butter
    45ml/3 tbsp sunflower oil
For the dressing
    30ml/2 tbsp fresh orange juice
    30ml/2 tbsp demerara (raw) sugar
    10ml/2 tsp soft green peppercorns
    salt
    fresh parsley, to garnish

1 Preheat the oven to 200°C/400°F/ Gas 6. Thickly peel the taros, making sure to remove all the skin as this can be an irritant. Cut into pieces about 5 x 2cm/2 x ¾in by 2cm/¾in, and place in a large bowl.

2 Peel the parsnips, halve lengthways and remove the inner core if necessary. Cut into the same size pieces as the taro and add to the bowl. Blanch in boiling water for 2 minutes and then drain. Peel or scrub the carrots, and halve or quarter them according to their size.

3 Place the butter and sunflower oil in a roasting pan and heat in the oven for 3–4 minutes. Add the vegetables, turning them in the oil to coat evenly. Roast in the oven for 30 minutes.

4 Meanwhile, blend the orange juice, sugar and soft green peppercorns in a small bowl. Remove the roasting pan from the oven and allow to cool for a minute or so and then carefully pour the mixture over the vegetables, stirring to coat them all. (If the liquid is poured on too soon the hot oil will spit.)

5 Return the pan to the oven and cook for a further 20 minutes or until the vegetables are crisp and golden. Then transfer to a warmed serving plate and sprinkle with a little salt. Garnish with fresh parsley to serve.

BAKED LEEKS WITH CHEESE AND YOGURT TOPPING

LIKE ALL VEGETABLES, THE FRESHER LEEKS ARE, THE BETTER THEIR FLAVOUR, AND THE FRESHEST LEEKS AVAILABLE SHOULD BE USED FOR THIS DISH. SMALL, YOUNG LEEKS ARE AROUND AT THE BEGINNING OF THE SEASON AND ARE PERFECT TO USE HERE.

SERVES FOUR

INGREDIENTS

8 small leeks, about 675g/1½lb
2 small (US medium) eggs or 1 large
  (US extra large) one, beaten
150g/5oz fresh goat's cheese
85ml/3fl oz/⅓ cup natural (plain)
  yogurt
50g/2oz Parmesan cheese, grated
25g/1oz/½ cup fresh white or brown
  breadcrumbs
salt and freshly ground black pepper

1 Preheat the oven to 180°C/350°F/ Gas 4 and butter a shallow ovenproof dish. Trim the leeks, cut a slit from top to bottom and rinse well under cold water.

2 Place the leeks in a pan of water, bring to the boil and simmer gently for 6–8 minutes until just tender. Remove and drain well using a slotted spoon, and arrange in the prepared dish.

3 Beat the beaten egg with the goat's cheese, yogurt and half the Parmesan cheese, and season well with salt and black pepper.

4 Pour the cheese and yogurt mixture over the leeks. Mix the breadcrumbs and remaining Parmesan cheese together and sprinkle over the sauce. Bake in the oven for 35–40 minutes until the top is crisp and golden brown.

ROAST ASPARAGUS CRÊPES

ASPARAGUS IS ALWAYS SPECIAL, EVEN WHEN SIMPLY STEAMED AND EATEN JUST AS IT IS. HOWEVER, FOR A REALLY SPLENDID APPETIZER, TRY THIS SIMPLE RECIPE. EITHER MAKE SIX LARGE OR TWELVE COCKTAIL-SIZE PANCAKES TO USE WITH SMALLER STEMS OF ASPARAGUS.

SERVES SIX

INGREDIENTS
    90–120ml/6–8 tbsp olive oil
    450g/1lb fresh asparagus
    175g/6oz/¾ cup mascarpone cheese
    60ml/4 tbsp single (light) cream
    25g/1oz Parmesan cheese, grated
    sea salt
For the pancakes
    175g/6oz 1½ cup plain (all-purpose)
      flour
    2 eggs
    350ml/12fl oz/1½ cups milk
    vegetable oil, for frying
    a pinch of salt

1 To make the pancake batter, mix the flour with the salt in a large bowl, food processor or blender, then add the eggs and milk and beat or process to make a smooth, fairly thin batter.

2 Heat a little oil in a large frying pan and add a small amount of batter, swirling the pan to coat the base evenly. Cook over a moderate heat for about 1 minute, then flip over and cook the other side until golden. Set aside and cook the rest of the pancakes in the same way; the mixture makes about six large or 12 smaller pancakes.

3 Preheat the oven to 180°C/350°F/ Gas 4 and lightly grease a large shallow ovenproof dish or roasting pan with some of the olive oil.

4 Trim the asparagus by placing on a board and cutting off the bases. Using a small sharp knife, peel away the woody ends, if necessary.

5 Arrange the asparagus in a single layer in the dish or pan, trickle over the remaining olive oil, rolling the asparagus to coat each one thoroughly. Sprinkle with salt and then roast in the oven for 8–12 minutes until tender (the cooking time depends on the stem thickness).

6 Blend the mascarpone cheese with the cream and Parmesan cheese and spread a generous tablespoonful over each of the pancakes, leaving a little for the topping. Preheat the grill (broiler).

7 Divide the asparagus spears among the pancakes, roll up and arrange in a single layer in an ovenproof dish. Spoon over the remaining cheese mixture and then place under a moderate grill for 4–5 minutes, until heated through and golden brown. Serve immediately.

BAKED ONIONS STUFFED <u>WITH</u> FETA

FETA CHEESE COMBINED WITH PINE NUTS AND FRESH CORIANDER MAKES A PIQUANT STUFFING WHICH OFFERS A WONDERFUL CONTRAST OF FLAVOUR WITH THE MELLOW RED ONION. FOR THE BEST TASTE MAKE SURE THAT YOU USE AUTHENTIC GREEK FETA CHEESE.

SERVES FOUR

INGREDIENTS
    4 large red onions
    15ml/1 tbsp olive oil
    25g/1oz/¼ cup pine nuts
    115g/4oz feta cheese, crumbled
    25g/1oz/½ cup white breadcrumbs
    15ml/1 tbsp chopped fresh coriander
    (cilantro)
    salt and freshly ground black pepper

1 Preheat the oven to 180°C/350°F/ Gas 4. Lightly grease a shallow ovenproof dish. Peel the onions and cut a thin slice from the top and base of each. Place in a large pan of boiling water and cook for 10–12 minutes until just tender. Drain on kitchen paper and leave to cool slightly.

2 Using a small knife or your fingers, remove the inner sections of the onions, leaving about two or three outer layers. Finely chop the inner sections and place the shells in the ovenproof dish.

3 Heat the oil in a medium-size frying pan and fry the chopped onions for 4–5 minutes until golden, then add the pine nuts and stir-fry for a few minutes.

4 Place the feta cheese in a small bowl and stir in the onions and pine nuts, the breadcrumbs and coriander. Season well with salt and pepper and then spoon the mixture into the onion shells. Cover loosely with foil and bake in the oven for about 30 minutes removing the foil for the last 10 minutes.

5 Serve as an appetizer or as a light lunch with warm olive bread.

ONION TARTS <u>WITH</u> GOAT'S CHEESE

A VARIATION OF A CLASSIC FRENCH DISH, TARTE À L'OIGNON, THIS DISH USES YOUNG GOAT'S CHEESE INSTEAD OF CREAM, AS IT IS MILD AND CREAMY AND COMPLEMENTS THE FLAVOUR OF THE ONIONS. THIS RECIPE MAKES EITHER EIGHT INDIVIDUAL TARTS OR ONE LARGE 23CM/9IN TART.

SERVES EIGHT

INGREDIENTS
For the pastry
    175g/6oz/1½ cups plain (all-purpose)
    flour
    65g/2½oz/generous ¼ cup butter
    25g/1oz goat's Cheddar or Cheddar
    cheese, grated
For the filling
    15–25ml/1–1½ tbsp olive or
    sunflower oil
    3 onions, finely sliced
    175g/6oz young goat's cheese
    2 eggs, beaten
    15ml/1 tbsp single (light) cream
    50g/2oz goat's Cheddar, grated
    15ml/1 tbsp chopped fresh tarragon
    salt and freshly ground black pepper

1 To make the pastry, sift the flour into a bowl and rub in the butter until the mixture resembles fine breadcrumbs. Stir in the cheese and add enough cold water to make a dough. Knead lightly, put in a plastic bag and chill.
Preheat the oven to 190°C/375°F/Gas 5.

2 Roll out the dough on a lightly floured surface, and then cut into eight rounds using a 11.5cm/4½in pastry cutter, and line eight 10cm/4in patty tins. Prick the bases with a fork and bake in the oven for 10–15 minutes until firm but not browned. Reduce the oven temperature to 180°C/350°F/Gas 4.

3 Heat the olive or sunflower oil in a large frying pan and fry the onions over a low heat for 20–25 minutes until they are a deep golden brown. Stir occasionally to prevent them burning.

4 Beat the goat's cheese with the eggs, cream, goat's Cheddar and tarragon. Season with salt and pepper and then stir in the fried onions.

5 Pour the mixture into the part-baked pastry cases and bake in the oven for 20–25 minutes until golden. Serve warm or cold with a green salad.

GREENS, BEANS AND PEAS

Greens are so good for us, we really should eat lots more. They're also versatile and quite delicious, so there's no excuse either! For a tasty accompaniment, beans and peas are the vegetables we first turn to. Podded peas are best when absolutely fresh, while corn is a delight, whether kept on the cob or served as kernels on the side.

HOT BROCCOLI TARTLETS

IN FRANCE, HOME OF THE CLASSIC QUICHE LORRAINE, YOU CAN FIND A WHOLE VARIETY OF SAVOURY TARTLETS, FILLED WITH ONIONS, LEEKS, MUSHROOMS AND BROCCOLI. THIS VERSION IS SIMPLE TO PREPARE AND WOULD MAKE AN ELEGANT START TO A MEAL.

MAKES EIGHT TO TEN

INGREDIENTS
    15ml/1 tbsp oil
    1 leek, finely sliced
    175g/6oz broccoli, broken into florets
    15g/½oz/1 tbsp butter
    15g/½oz/2 tbsp plain (all-purpose) flour
    150ml/¼ pint/⅔ cup milk
    50g/2oz goat's Cheddar or farmhouse
      Cheddar, grated
    salt and freshly ground black pepper
    fresh chervil, to garnish
For the pastry
    175g/6oz/1½ cups plain (all-purpose) flour
    75g/3oz/6 tbsp butter
    1 egg

1 To make the pastry, place the flour and a pinch of salt in a bowl. Rub in the butter. Add the egg to make a dough, using a little cold water if necessary. Knead lightly, wrap in clear film (plastic wrap) and rest in the refrigerator for 1 hour.

2 Preheat the oven to 190°C/375°F/ Gas 5. Let the dough return to room temperature for 10 minutes and then roll out on a lightly floured surface and line 8–10 deep patty tins. Prick the bases with a fork and bake in the oven for about 10–15 minutes until the pastry is firm and lightly golden. Increase the oven temperature to 200°C/400°F/Gas 6.

3 Heat the oil in a small pan and sauté the leek for 4–5 minutes until soft. Add the broccoli, and stir-fry for about 1 minute, then add a little water. Cover and steam for 3–4 minutes until the broccoli is just tender.

4 Melt the butter in a separate pan, stir in the flour and cook for a minute, stirring all the time. Slowly add the milk and stir to make a smooth sauce. Add half of the cheese and season with salt and pepper.

5 Spoon a little broccoli and leek into each tartlet case and then spoon over the sauce. Sprinkle each tartlet with the remaining cheese and then bake in the oven for about 10 minutes until golden.

6 Serve the tartlets as part of a buffet or as an appetizer, garnished with chervil.

CHARD PASTIES

LIKE SPINACH, CHARD GOES PARTICULARLY WELL IN PASTIES. UNLIKE SOME GREEN VEGETABLES, IT CAN SURVIVE A LITTLE EXTRA COOKING AND IS SUBSTANTIAL ENOUGH TO BE THE PRINCIPAL INGREDIENT IN A DISH. FOR A MORE FLAVOURSOME PASTRY, REPLACE A LITTLE OF THE BUTTER WITH GRATED CHEESE.

SERVES FOUR

INGREDIENTS
  675g/1½lb Swiss chard
  25g/1oz/2 tbsp butter or margarine
  1 onion, finely chopped
  75g/3oz streaky (fatty) bacon, chopped
  50g/2oz Gruyère cheese, grated
  25g/1oz/½ cup fresh brown or white
    breadcrumbs
  90ml/6 tbsp single (light) cream
  salt and freshly ground black pepper
For the pastry
  275g/10oz/2½ cups plain (all-
    purpose) flour
  150g/5oz/generous ½ cup butter or
    margarine
  beaten egg, for glazing

1 To make the pastry, place the flour and salt in a mixing bowl and rub in the butter or margarine. Add a little cold water and mix to a soft dough. Knead lightly on a floured surface. Wrap in clear film (plastic wrap) and chill for 30 minutes.

2 Trim the stalks of the chard and then chop both the leaves and stalks. Place in a heavy pan, cover and cook over a low heat for 6–8 minutes until the stalks are tender and the leaves wilted, shaking the pan occasionally. Strain, then press out the excess liquid, place in a mixing bowl and leave to cool.

3 Melt the butter in a small frying pan and fry the onion and bacon for about 4–5 minutes until the onion is lightly golden and the bacon browned.

4 Add the onion and bacon to the chard and stir in the cheese, breadcrumbs, cream and seasoning to taste. Preheat the oven to 200°C/400°F/Gas 6.

5 Divide the pastry into four and roll out into rounds. Spoon the filling on to the centre of each and dampen the edges with water. Bring the sides together over the filling and press together to seal. Brush with beaten egg and then put on an oiled baking sheet. Bake for about 15–20 minutes until the pastry is golden.

CAULIFLOWER AND MUSHROOM GOUGÈRE

THIS IS AN ALL-ROUND FAVOURITE VEGETARIAN DISH. WHEN COOKING IT FOR MEAT LOVERS, CHOPPED ROAST HAM OR FRIED BACON CAN BE ADDED.

SERVES FOUR TO SIX

INGREDIENTS
300ml/½ pint/1¼ cups water
115g/4oz/½ cup butter or margarine
150g/5oz/1¼ cups plain (all-purpose) flour
4 eggs
115g/4oz Gruyère or Cheddar cheese, finely diced
5ml/1 tsp Dijon mustard
salt and freshly ground black pepper
For the filling
½ x 400g/14oz can tomatoes
15ml/1 tbsp sunflower oil
15g/½oz/1 tbsp butter or margarine
1 onion, chopped
115g/4oz button (white) mushrooms, halved if large
1 small cauliflower, broken into small florets
a sprig of thyme
salt and freshly ground black pepper

1 Preheat the oven to 200°C/400°F/ Gas 6 and butter a large ovenproof dish. Place the water and butter together in a large pan and heat until the butter has melted. Remove from the heat and add all the flour at once. Beat well with a wooden spoon for about 30 seconds until smooth. Allow to cool slightly.

2 Beat in the eggs, one at a time, and continue beating until the mixture is thick and glossy. Stir in the cheese and mustard and season with salt and pepper. Spread the mixture around the sides of the ovenproof dish, leaving a hollow in the centre for the filling.

3 To make the filling, purée the tomatoes in a blender or food processor and then pour into a measuring jug (cup). Add enough water to make up to 300ml/½ pint/1¼ cups of liquid.

4 Heat the oil and butter in a flameproof casserole and fry the onion for about 3–4 minutes until softened but not browned. Add the mushrooms and cook for 2–3 minutes until they begin to be flecked with brown. Add the cauliflower florets and stir-fry for 1 minute.

5 Add the tomato liquid, thyme and seasoning. Cook, uncovered, over a gentle heat for about 5 minutes until the cauliflower is only just tender.

6 Spoon the mixture into the hollow in the ovenproof dish, adding all the liquid with it. Bake in the oven for about 35–40 minutes, until the outer pastry is well risen and golden brown.

COOK'S TIP
For a variation, ham or bacon can be added. Use about 115–150g/4–5oz thickly sliced roast ham and add to the sauce at the end of step 5.

SPINACH <u>IN</u> FILO <u>WITH</u> THREE CHEESES

THIS IS A GOOD CHOICE TO SERVE WHEN VEGETARIANS AND MEAT EATERS ARE GATHERED TOGETHER FOR A MEAL AS, WHATEVER THEIR PREFERENCE, EVERYONE SEEMS PARTIAL TO THIS TASTY DISH.

SERVES FOUR

INGREDIENTS

    450g/1lb spinach
    15ml/1 tbsp sunflower oil
    15g/½oz/1 tbsp butter
    1 small onion, finely chopped
    175g/6oz ricotta cheese
    115g/4oz/¾ cup feta cheese, cut into
      small cubes
    75g/3oz Gruyère or Emmenthal
      cheese, grated
    15ml/1 tbsp fresh chopped chervil
    5ml/1 tsp fresh chopped marjoram
    5 large or 10 small sheets filo pastry
    40–50g/1½–2oz butter, melted
    salt and freshly ground black pepper

1 Preheat the oven to 190°C/375°F/Gas 5. Cook the spinach in a large pan over a moderate heat for 3–4 minutes until the leaves have wilted, shaking the pan occasionally. Strain and press out the excess liquid.

2 Heat the oil and butter in a pan and fry the onion for 3–4 minutes until softened. Remove from the heat and add half of the spinach. Combine, using a metal spoon to break up the spinach.

3 Add the ricotta cheese and stir until evenly combined. Stir in the remaining spinach, again chopping it into the mixture with a metal spoon. Fold in the feta and Gruyère or Emmenthal cheese, the chervil, marjoram and seasoning.

4 Lay a sheet of filo pastry measuring 30cm/12 in square on a work surface. (If you have small filo sheets, lay them side by side, and overlapping by about 2.5cm/1in in the middle.) Brush with melted butter and cover with a second sheet; brush this with butter and build up five layers of pastry in this way.

5 Spread the filling over the pastry, leaving a 2.5cm/1in border. Fold the sides inwards and then roll up.

6 Place the roll, seam side down, on a greased baking sheet and brush with the remaining butter. Bake in the oven for about 30 minutes until golden brown.

PAK CHOI WITH LIME DRESSING

FOR THIS THAI RECIPE, THE COCONUT DRESSING IS TRADITIONALLY MADE USING FISH SAUCE, BUT VEGETARIANS COULD USE MUSHROOM KETCHUP INSTEAD. BEWARE, THIS IS A FIERY DISH!

SERVES FOUR

INGREDIENTS

6 spring onions (scallions)
2 pak choi (bok choy)
30ml/2 tbsp oil
3 fresh red chillies, cut into
  thin strips
4 garlic cloves, thinly sliced
15ml/1 tbsp crushed peanuts
For the dressing
15–30ml/1–2 tbsp fish sauce
30ml/2 tbsp lime juice
250ml/8fl oz/1 cup coconut milk

1 To make the dressing, blend together the fish sauce and lime juice, and then stir in the coconut milk.

2 Cut the spring onions diagonally into slices, including all but the very tips of the green parts.

3 Using a large sharp knife, cut the pak choi into very fine shreds.

4 Heat the oil in a wok and stir-fry the chillies for 2–3 minutes until crisp. Transfer to a plate using a slotted spoon.

5 Stir-fry the garlic for 30–60 seconds until golden brown and transfer to the plate with the chillies.

6 Stir-fry the white parts of the spring onions for about 2–3 minutes and then add the green parts and stir-fry for a further 1 minute. Add to the plate with the chillies and garlic.

7 Bring a large pan of salted water to the boil and add the pak choi; stir twice and then drain immediately.

8 Place the warmed pak choi in a large bowl, add the coconut dressing and stir well. Spoon into a large serving bowl and sprinkle with the crushed peanuts and the stir-fried chilli mixture. Serve either warm or cold.

COOK'S TIP
Coconut milk is available in cans from large supermarkets and Chinese stores. Alternatively, creamed coconut is available in packets. To use creamed coconut, place 115g/4oz/½ cup in a jug and pour over 250ml/8fl oz/1 cup boiling water. Stir well until dissolved.

DOLMADES

A traditional Greek dish, dolmades are stuffed vine leaves. If you can't obtain fresh vine leaves, use a packet of brined vine leaves. Soak the leaves in hot water for 10 minutes then rinse and dry well on kitchen paper before use.

MAKES 20–24

INGREDIENTS

20–30 fresh young vine leaves
30ml/2 tbsp olive oil
1 large onion, finely chopped
1 garlic clove, crushed
225g/8oz/3 cups cooked long grain
  rice, or mixed white and wild rice
about 45ml/3 tbsp pine nuts
15ml/1 tbsp flaked (sliced) almonds
40g/1½oz/generous ¼ cup sultanas
  (golden raisins)
15ml/1 tbsp chopped chives
15ml/1 tbsp finely chopped fresh mint
juice of ½ lemon
150ml/¼ pint/⅔ cup white wine
hot vegetable stock
salt and freshly ground black pepper
sprig of mint, to garnish
Greek (US strained plain) yogurt,
  to serve

1 Bring a large pan of water to the boil then cook the vine leaves for about 2–3 minutes. They will darken and go limp after about 1 minute and simmering for a further minute or so ensures they are pliable. If using leaves from a packet, place them in a large bowl, cover with boiling water and leave for a few minutes until the leaves can be easily separated. Rinse them under cold water and drain on kitchen paper.

2 Heat the oil in a small frying pan and fry the onion and garlic for 3–4 minutes over a gentle heat until soft.

3 Spoon the onion and garlic mixture into a bowl and add the cooked rice.

4 Stir in 30ml/2 tbsp of the pine nuts, the almonds, sultanas, chives, mint, lemon juice and seasoning and mix well.

5 Lay a vine leaf on a clean surface, with veined side uppermost. Place a spoonful of filling near the stem, fold the lower part of the leaf over it and roll up, folding in the sides as you go. Continue stuffing the vine leaves in this way.

6 Line the base of a deep frying pan with four large vine leaves. Place the stuffed vine leaves close together in the pan, seam side down, in a single layer.

7 Add the wine and enough stock just to cover the vine leaves. Now place a plate directly over the leaves, then cover and simmer gently for 30 minutes, checking to make sure the pan does not boil dry.

8 Chill the vine leaves, then serve garnished with the remaining pine nuts, a sprig of mint and a little yogurt.

CORN AND SCALLOP CHOWDER

FRESH HOME-GROWN CORN IS IDEAL FOR THIS CHOWDER, ALTHOUGH CANNED OR FROZEN ALSO WORK WELL. THIS SOUP IS ALMOST A MEAL IN ITSELF AND MAKES A PERFECT LUNCH DISH.

SERVES FOUR TO SIX

INGREDIENTS

2 ears of corn or 200g/7oz frozen
   or canned corn
600ml/1 pint/2½ cups milk
15g/½oz/ 1 tbsp butter or margarine
1 small leek or onion, chopped
40g/1½oz smoked streaky (fatty)
   bacon, finely chopped
1 small garlic clove, crushed
1 small green (bell) pepper, seeded
   and diced
1 celery stick, chopped
1 medium potato, diced
15ml/1 tbsp plain (all-purpose) flour
300ml/½ pint/1¼ cups chicken
   or vegetable stock
4 scallops
115g/4oz cooked fresh mussels
a pinch of paprika
150ml/¼ pint/⅔ cup single (light)
   cream (optional)
salt and freshly ground black pepper

1 Slice down the ears of fresh corn to remove the kernels; thaw frozen corn and drain and rinse canned corn. Place half of the kernels in a food processor and process with a little of the milk.

2 Melt the butter or margarine in a large pan and gently fry the leek or onion, bacon and garlic for 4–5 minutes until the leek or onion is soft but not browned. Add the green pepper, celery and potato; sweat over a gentle heat for a further 3–4 minutes, stirring frequently.

3 Stir in the flour and cook for about 1–2 minutes until the mixture is golden and frothy. Gradually stir in the milk and corn mixture, stock, the remaining milk and corn kernels and seasoning.

4 Bring to the boil and then reduce the heat to a gentle simmer, and cook, partially covered, for 15–20 minutes until the vegetables are tender.

5 Pull the corals away from the scallops and slice the white flesh into 5mm/¼in slices. Stir the scallops into the soup, cook for 4 minutes and then stir in the corals, mussels and paprika. Allow to heat through for a few minutes and then stir in the cream, if using. Adjust the seasoning to taste and serve.

MANGETOUTS WITH CHICKEN AND GINGER

MANGETOUTS ARE SO DELICATE AND FRESH-TASTING THAT IT SEEMS A CRIME TO DO ANYTHING AT ALL WITH THEM, BARRING FLASH COOKING AND SERVING THEM HOT OR COLD WITH A LITTLE BUTTER OR A VINAIGRETTE DRESSING. HOWEVER, THEY ARE EXCELLENT IN STIR-FRIES, ADDING COLOUR AND TEXTURE.

SERVES FOUR

INGREDIENTS

4 skinless chicken breast fillets
225g/8oz mangetouts (snow peas)
45ml/3 tbsp vegetable oil, plus
  oil, for deep frying
3 garlic cloves, finely chopped
2.5cm/1in piece fresh root ginger,
  freshly grated
5–6 spring onions (scallions), cut into
  4cm/1½in lengths
10ml/2 tsp sesame oil
For the marinade
5ml/1 tsp cornflour (cornstarch)
15ml/1 tbsp light soy sauce
15ml/1 tbsp medium dry sherry
15ml/1 tbsp vegetable oil
For the sauce
5ml/1 tsp cornflour (cornstarch)
10–15ml/2–3 tsp dark soy sauce
120ml/4fl oz/½ cup chicken stock
30ml/2 tbsp oyster sauce
boiled rice, to serve

1 Cut the chicken into strips about 1 x 4cm/½ x 1½in. For the marinade, blend together the cornflour and soy sauce. Stir in the sherry and oil. Pour over the chicken, turning the pieces over to coat evenly, and leave for 30 minutes.

2 Trim the mangetouts and plunge into a pan of boiling salted water. Bring back to the boil and then drain and refresh them under cold running water.

3 To make the sauce, mix together the cornflour, soy sauce, stock and oyster sauce and set aside.

4 Heat the oil in a deep fryer. Drain the chicken strips and fry, in batches if necessary, for about 30 seconds to brown. Drain and transfer to a plate using a slotted spoon.

5 Heat 15ml/1 tbsp of the vegetable oil in a wok and add the garlic and ginger. Stir-fry for about 30 seconds. Add the mangetouts and stir-fry for 1–2 minutes. Transfer to a plate and keep warm.

6 Heat the remaining vegetable oil in the wok, add the spring onions and stir-fry for 1–2 minutes. Add the chicken and stir-fry for 2 minutes. Pour in the sauce, reduce the heat and cook until it thickens and the chicken is cooked through.

7 Stir in the sesame oil, and pour over the mangetouts. Serve with boiled rice.

PEAS WITH BABY ONIONS AND CREAM

IDEALLY, USE FRESH PEAS AND FRESH BABY ONIONS. FROZEN PEAS ARE AN ACCEPTABLE SUBSTITUTE IF FRESH ONES AREN'T AVAILABLE, BUT FROZEN ONIONS TEND TO BE INSIPID AND ARE NOT WORTH USING. ALTERNATIVELY, USE THE WHITE PARTS OF SPRING ONIONS.

SERVES FOUR

INGREDIENTS

   175g/6oz baby (pearl) onions
   15g/½ oz/1 tbsp butter
   900g/2lb fresh peas (about
     350g/12oz shelled or frozen)
   150ml/¼ pint/⅔ cup double (heavy)
     cream
   15g/½oz/2 tbsp plain (all-purpose)
     flour
   10ml/2 tsp chopped fresh parsley
   15–30ml/1–2 tbsp lemon juice
     (optional)
   salt and freshly ground black pepper

1 Peel the onions and halve them if necessary. Then melt the butter in a flameproof casserole. Fry the onions for 5–6 minutes over a moderate heat, until they begin to be flecked with brown.

2 Add the peas and stir-fry for a few minutes. Add 120ml/4fl oz/¼ cup water and bring to the boil. Partially cover and simmer for about 10 minutes until both the peas and onions are tender. There should be a thin layer of water on the base of the pan – add a little more water if necessary or, if there is too much liquid, remove the lid and increase the heat until the liquid is reduced.

3 Using a small whisk, blend the cream with the flour. Remove the pan from the heat and stir in the combined cream and flour, parsley and seasoning to taste.

4 Cook over a gentle heat for about 3–4 minutes, until the sauce is thick. Taste and adjust the seasoning; add a little lemon juice to sharpen, if liked.

FRENCH BEANS WITH BACON AND CREAM

SERVES FOUR

INGREDIENTS

350g/12oz French (green) beans
50–75g/2–3oz bacon, chopped
25g/1oz/2 tbsp butter or margarine
15ml/1 tbsp plain (all-purpose) flour
350ml/12fl oz/1½ cups milk
  and single (light) cream, mixed
salt and freshly ground black pepper

1 Preheat the oven to 190°C/375°F/ Gas 5. Trim the beans and cook in lightly salted boiling water for about 5 minutes until just tender. Drain and place them in an ovenproof dish.

2 Dry-fry the bacon until crisp, crumble into very small pieces and stir into the beans in the dish.

3 Melt the butter or margarine in a pan, stir in the flour and then add the milk and cream mixture to make a smooth sauce. Season well with salt and ground black pepper.

4 Pour the sauce over the beans and carefully mix it in. Cover lightly with a piece of foil and bake in the oven for 15–20 minutes until hot.

MUSHROOMS
AND SQUASHES

Nearly everyone has a favourite mushroom dish. Mushrooms

have the ability to go with almost anything, which is why there

is always such a range of dishes when it comes to these fungi.

Squashes are bright and colourful autumn vegetables.

Locally grown courgettes are available from mid- to late

summer. Marrows follow in late summer and then come

the winter squashes — onion squashes and pumpkins —

just in time for Hallowe'en.

CREAM OF MUSHROOM SOUP

A GOOD MUSHROOM SOUP MAKES THE MOST OF THE SUBTLE AND SOMETIMES RATHER ELUSIVE FLAVOUR OF MUSHROOMS. BUTTON MUSHROOMS ARE USED HERE FOR THEIR PALE COLOUR; CHESTNUT OR, BETTER STILL, FIELD MUSHROOMS GIVE A FULLER FLAVOUR BUT TURN THE SOUP BROWN.

SERVES FOUR

INGREDIENTS
    275g/10oz/3¾ cups
      button (white) mushrooms
    15ml/1 tbsp sunflower oil
    40g/1½oz/3 tbsp butter
    1 small onion, finely chopped
    15ml/1 tbsp plain (all-purpose) flour
    450ml/¾ pint/1¾ cups vegetable stock
    450ml/¾ pint/1¾ cups milk
    pinch of dried basil
    30–45ml/2–3 tbsp single (light) cream
    salt and freshly ground black pepper
    fresh basil leaves, to garnish

1 Separate the mushroom caps from the stalks. Finely slice the caps and finely chop the stalks.

2 Heat the oil and half the butter in a heavy pan and add the onion, mushroom stalks and half of the sliced mushroom caps. Fry for about 1–2 minutes, stirring frequently, and then cover and sweat over a gentle heat for 6–7 minutes, stirring occasionally.

3 Stir in the flour and cook for about 1 minute. Gradually add the stock and milk, to make a smooth thin sauce. Add the basil, and season with salt and pepper. Bring to the boil and then simmer, partly covered, for 15 minutes.

4 Cool slightly and then pour the soup into a food processor or blender and process until smooth. Melt the rest of the butter in a frying pan and fry the remaining mushrooms caps gently for 3–4 minutes until they are just tender.

5 Pour the soup into a clean pan and stir in the sliced mushrooms. Heat until very hot and adjust the seasoning. Add a little cream and serve sprinkled with fresh basil leaves.

SOUFFLÉ OMELETTE WITH MUSHROOM SAUCE

A SOUFFLÉ OMELETTE INVOLVES A LITTLE MORE PREPARATION THAN AN ORDINARY OMELETTE BUT THE RESULT IS LIGHT YET SATISFYINGLY FILLING.

SERVES ONE

INGREDIENTS
    2 eggs, separated
    15g/½oz/1 tbsp butter
    sprig of parsley
For the mushroom sauce
    15g/½oz/1 tbsp butter
    75g/3oz/generous 1 cup button
      (white) mushrooms, thinly sliced
    15ml/1 tbsp plain (all-purpose) flour
    85–120ml/3–4fl oz/½ cup milk
    5ml/1 tsp chopped fresh parsley
      (optional)
    salt and freshly ground black pepper

1 To make the mushroom sauce, melt the butter in a pan or frying pan and fry the thinly sliced mushrooms for 4–5 minutes until tender.

2 Stir in the flour and then gradually add the milk, stirring all the time, to make a smooth sauce. Add the parsley, if using, and season with salt and pepper. Keep warm to one side.

3 Beat the egg yolks with 15ml/1 tbsp water and season with a little salt and pepper. Whisk the egg whites until stiff and then fold into the egg yolks using a metal spoon. Preheat the grill (broiler).

4 Melt the butter in a large frying pan and pour the egg mixture into the pan. Cook over a gentle heat for 2–4 minutes. Place the frying pan under the grill and cook for a further 3–4 minutes until the top is golden brown.

5 Slide the omelette on to a warmed serving plate, pour over the mushroom sauce and fold the omelette in half. Serve garnished with a sprig of parsley.

TAGLIATELLE FUNGI

THE MUSHROOM SAUCE IS QUICK TO MAKE AND THE PASTA COOKS VERY QUICKLY; BOTH NEED TO BE COOKED AS NEAR TO SERVING AS POSSIBLE SO CAREFUL COORDINATION IS REQUIRED. PUT THE PASTA IN TO COOK WHEN THE CRÈME FRAÎCHE IS ADDED TO THE SAUCE.

SERVES FOUR

INGREDIENTS
    about 50g/2oz/4 tbsp butter
    225–350g/8–12oz chanterelles
      or other wild mushrooms
    15ml/1 tbsp plain (all-purpose) flour
    150ml/¼ pint/⅔ cup milk
    90ml/6 tbsp crème fraîche
    15ml/1 tbsp chopped fresh parsley
    275g/10oz fresh tagliatelle
    olive oil
    salt and freshly ground black pepper

3 Add the crème fraîche, parsley, mushrooms and seasoning, and stir well. Cook very gently to heat through and then keep warm while cooking the pasta.

4 Cook the pasta in a large pan of boiling water for about 4–5 minutes (or according to the instructions on the packet). Drain well, toss in a little olive oil then turn on to a warmed serving plate. Pour the mushroom sauce over and serve immediately.

COOK'S TIP
Chanterelles are a little tricky to wash, as they are so delicate. However, since these are woodland mushrooms, it's important to clean them thoroughly. Hold each one by the stalk and let cold water run under the gills to dislodge hidden dirt. Shake gently to dry.

1 Melt 40g/1½oz/3 tbsp of the butter in a frying pan and fry the mushrooms for about 2–3 minutes over a gentle heat until the juices begin to run. Increase the heat and cook until the liquid has almost evaporated. Transfer the mushrooms to a bowl using a slotted spoon.

2 Stir in the flour, adding a little more butter if necessary, and cook for about 1 minute, and then gradually stir in the milk to make a smooth sauce.

SHIITAKE FRIED RICE

THESE MUSHROOMS HAVE A STRONG, MEATY MUSHROOMY AROMA AND FLAVOUR. THIS IS A VERY EASY RECIPE TO MAKE, AND ALTHOUGH IT IS A SIDE DISH IT COULD ALMOST BE A MEAL IN ITSELF.

SERVES FOUR

INGREDIENTS
- 2 eggs
- 45ml/3 tbsp vegetable oil
- 350g/12oz shiitake mushrooms
- 8 spring onions (scallions), sliced diagonally
- 1 garlic clove, crushed
- ½ green (bell) pepper, chopped
- 25g/1oz/2 tbsp butter
- 175–225g/6–8oz/about 1 cup long grain rice, cooked
- 15ml/1 tbsp medium dry sherry
- 30ml/2 tbsp dark soy sauce
- 15ml/1 tbsp chopped fresh coriander (cilantro)
- salt

1 Beat the eggs with 15ml/1 tbsp cold water and season with a little salt.

2 Heat 15ml/1 tbsp of the oil in a wok or large frying pan, pour in the eggs and cook to make a large omelette. Lift the sides of the omelette and tilt the wok so that the uncooked egg can run under the cooked egg. When done, roll up the omelette and slice thinly.

3 Remove and discard the mushroom stalks if tough and slice the caps thinly, halving them if they are large.

4 Heat 15ml/1 tbsp of the remaining oil in the wok and stir-fry the spring onions and garlic for 3–4 minutes until softened but not brown. Transfer them to a plate using a slotted spoon.

5 Add the pepper, stir-fry for about 2–3 minutes, then add the butter and the remaining 15ml/1 tbsp of oil. As the butter begins to sizzle, add the sliced mushrooms and stir-fry over a moderate heat for 3–4 minutes until soft.

6 Loosen the rice grains as much as possible. Pour the sherry over the mushrooms and then stir in the rice.

7 Heat the rice over a moderate heat, stirring all the time to prevent it sticking. If the rice seems very dry, add a little more oil. Stir in the reserved onions and omelette slices, the soy sauce and coriander. Cook for a few minutes until heated through, then serve.

COOK'S TIP
Unlike risotto, for which rice is cooked along with the other ingredients, Chinese fried rice is always made using cooked rice. If you use 175–225g/6–8oz uncooked long grain, you will get about 450–500g/16–20oz cooked rice, enough for four people.

STUFFED MUSHROOMS

THIS IS A CLASSIC MUSHROOM DISH, STRONGLY FLAVOURED WITH GARLIC. USE FLAT MUSHROOMS OR FIELD MUSHROOMS THAT ARE SOMETIMES AVAILABLE FROM FARM SHOPS.

SERVES FOUR

INGREDIENTS

- 450g/1lb large flat mushrooms
- butter, for greasing
- about 75ml/5 tbsp olive oil
- 2 garlic cloves, minced (ground) or very finely chopped
- 45ml/3 tbsp/¾-1 cup finely chopped fresh parsley
- 40–50g/1½–2oz fresh white breadcrumbs
- salt and freshly ground black pepper
- sprig of flat leaf parsley, to garnish

1 Preheat the oven to 180°C/350°F/ Gas 4. Cut off the mushroom stalks and reserve them.

2 Arrange the mushroom caps in a buttered shallow dish, gill side upwards.

3 Heat 15ml/1 tbsp of oil in a frying pan and fry the garlic briefly. Finely chop the mushroom stalks; mix with the parsley and breadcrumbs. Add the garlic, salt and pepper and 15ml/1tbsp of the oil. Pile a little mixture on each mushroom.

4 Add the remaining oil to the dish and cover the mushrooms with buttered greaseproof paper. Bake for about 15–20 minutes, removing the paper for the last 5 minutes to brown the tops. Garnish with a sprig of flat leaf parsley.

COOK'S TIP
The cooking time for the mushrooms depends on their size and thickness. If they are fairly thin, cook for slightly less time. They should be tender but not too soft when they are cooked. If a stronger garlic flavour is preferred, do not cook the garlic before combining it with the breadcrumb mixture.

LOOFAH AND AUBERGINE RATATOUILLE

LOOFAHS HAVE A SIMILAR FLAVOUR TO COURGETTES AND CONSEQUENTLY TASTE EXCELLENT WITH AUBERGINES AND TOMATOES. UNLESS USING VERY YOUNG LOOFAHS, WHICH ARE BEST, ENSURE THAT YOU PEEL AWAY THE ROUGH SKIN, AS IT CAN BE SHARP.

SERVES FOUR

INGREDIENTS
- 1 large or 2 medium aubergines (eggplants)
- 450g/1lb young loofahs or sponge gourds
- 1 large red (bell) pepper, cut into large chunks
- 225g/8oz cherry tomatoes
- 225g/8oz shallots, peeled
- 10ml/2 tsp ground coriander
- 60ml/4 tbsp olive oil
- 2 garlic cloves, finely chopped
- a few coriander (cilantro) leaves
- salt and freshly ground black pepper

1 Cut the aubergine into thick chunks and sprinkle the pieces with salt. Set aside in a colander for about 45 minutes and then rinse well under cold running water and pat dry.

2 Preheat the oven to 220°C/425°F/ Gas 7. Slice the loofahs into 2cm/¾in pieces. Place the aubergine, loofah and pepper pieces, together with the tomatoes and shallots in a roasting pan which is large enough to take all the vegetables in a single layer.

3 Sprinkle with the ground coriander and olive oil and then scatter over the chopped garlic and coriander leaves. Season to taste.

4 Roast for about 25 minutes, stirring the vegetables occasionally, until the loofah is golden brown and the peppers are beginning to char at the edges. Stir, then place in a warmed serving dish.

BAKED COURGETTES

THIS RECIPE IS PARTICULARLY DELICIOUS WHEN VERY SMALL AND VERY FRESH COURGETTES ARE USED.
THE CREAMY YET TANGY GOAT'S CHEESE PROVIDES AN EXCELLENT CONTRAST WITH THE DELICATE
FLAVOUR OF THE YOUNG COURGETTES.

SERVES FOUR

INGREDIENTS

  8 small courgettes (zucchini), about
    450g/1lb total weight
  15ml/1 tbsp olive oil, plus extra
    for greasing
  75–115g/3–4oz goat's cheese, cut
    into thin strips
  a small bunch fresh mint, finely
    chopped
  freshly ground black pepper

1 Preheat the oven to 180°C/350°F/
Gas 4. Cut out eight rectangles of foil
large enough to encase each courgette
and brush each with a little oil.

2 Trim the courgettes and cut a thin slit
along the length of each.

3 Insert pieces of goat's cheese in the
slits. Add a little mint and sprinkle with
the olive oil and black pepper.

4 Wrap each courgette in the foil
rectangles, place on a baking sheet and
bake for about 25 minutes until tender.

COOK'S TIP
Almost any cheese could be used in this
recipe. Mild cheeses, however, such as a
mild Cheddar or mozzarella, will best
allow the flavour of the courgettes to
be appreciated to their full.

BAKED MARROW WITH CREAM AND PARSLEY

THIS IS A REALLY GLORIOUS WAY WITH A SIMPLE AND MODEST VEGETABLE. TRY TO FIND A SMALL, FIRM AND UNBLEMISHED MARROW FOR THIS RECIPE, AS THE FLAVOUR WILL BE SWEET, FRESH AND DELICATE. YOUNG MARROWS DO NOT NEED PEELING; MORE MATURE ONES DO.

SERVES FOUR

INGREDIENTS
- 1 small young marrow (large zucchini), about 900g/2lb
- 30ml/2 tbsp olive oil
- 15g/½oz/1 tbsp butter
- 1 onion, chopped
- 15ml/1 tbsp plain (all-purpose) flour
- 300ml/½ pint/1¼ cups milk and single (light) cream mixed
- 30ml/2 tbsp chopped fresh parsley
- salt and freshly ground black pepper

1 Preheat the oven to 180°C/350°F/ Gas 4 and cut the marrow into pieces measuring about 5 x 2.5cm/2 x 1in.

2 Heat the oil and butter in a flameproof casserole and fry the onion over a gentle heat until very soft.

3 Add the marrow and sauté for 1–2 minutes and then stir in the flour. Cook for a few minutes, then stir in the milk and cream mixture.

4 Add the parsley and seasoning, stir well and then cover and cook in the oven for 30–35 minutes. If you like, remove the lid for the final 5 minutes of cooking to brown the top. Alternatively, serve the marrow in its rich pale sauce.

COOK'S TIP
Chopped fresh basil or a mixture of basil and chervil also tastes good in this dish.

ONION SQUASH RISOTTO

THIS RISOTTO PROVIDES A WARM AND COMFORTING MEAL AFTER A TIRING DAY. FOR A VEGETARIAN ALTERNATIVE SIMPLY OMIT THE BACON AND USE VEGETABLE STOCK.

SERVES FOUR

INGREDIENTS
    1 onion squash or pumpkin, about
      900g–1kg/2–2¼lb
    30ml/2 tbsp olive oil
    1 onion, chopped
    1–2 garlic cloves, crushed
    115g/4oz streaky (fatty) bacon,
      chopped
    115g/4oz/generous ½ cup arborio rice
    600–750ml/1–1¼ pints/2½–3 cups
      chicken stock
    40g/1½oz Parmesan cheese, grated
    15ml/1 tbsp chopped fresh parsley
    salt and freshly ground black pepper

1 Halve or quarter the onion squash or pumpkin, remove the seeds and skin, and then cut into chunks about 1–2cm/ ½–¾in in size.

2 Heat the oil in a flameproof casserole and fry the onion and garlic for about 3–4 minutes, stirring frequently. Add the bacon and continue frying until both the onion and bacon are lightly golden.

3 Add the squash or pumpkin, stir-fry for a few minutes. Add the rice and cook for about 2 minutes, stirring all the time.

4 Pour in about half of the stock and season. Stir well and then half cover and simmer gently for about 20 minutes, stirring occasionally. As the liquid is absorbed, add more stock and stir to prevent the mixture sticking to the base.

5 When the squash and rice are nearly tender, add a little more stock. Cook, uncovered for 5–10 minutes. Stir in the Parmesan cheese and parsley and serve.

PUMPKIN SOUP

THE SWEET FLAVOUR OF PUMPKIN IS GOOD IN SOUPS, TEAMING WELL WITH OTHER MORE SAVOURY INGREDIENTS SUCH AS ONIONS AND POTATOES TO MAKE A MILD AND SOOTHING DISH.

SERVES FOUR TO SIX

INGREDIENTS
    15ml/1 tbsp sunflower oil
    25g/1oz/2 tbsp butter
    1 large onion, sliced
    675g/1½lb pumpkin, cut into
      large chunks
    450g/1lb potatoes, sliced
    600ml/1 pint/2½ cups vegetable stock
    a good pinch of nutmeg
    5ml/1 tsp chopped fresh tarragon
    600ml/1 pint/2½ cups milk
    about 5–10ml/1–2 tsp lemon juice
    salt and freshly ground black pepper

1 Heat the oil and butter in a heavy pan and fry the onion for 4–5 minutes over a gentle heat until soft but not browned, stirring frequently.

2 Add the pumpkin and potato, stir well and then cover and sweat over a low heat for about 10 minutes until the vegetables are almost tender, stirring occasionally to prevent them from sticking to the pan.

3 Stir in the stock, nutmeg, tarragon and seasoning. Bring to the boil and then simmer for about 10 minutes until the vegetables are completely tender.

4 Allow to cool slightly, then pour into a food processor or blender and pureé until smooth. Pour back into a clean pan and add the milk. Heat gently and then taste, adding the lemon juice and extra seasoning if necessary. Serve piping hot with crusty brown bread.

SALAD
VEGETABLES

A salad can be just a few leaves tossed in a simple

dressing, but there are plenty of more exciting

possibilities. Chicken Livers and Green Salad or Warm

Duck Salad with Orange would make an excellent

lunch or supper dish. If you just want a side salad or

a light first course, you could try Radish, Mango and

Apple Salad or the Rocket and Grilled Chèvre Salad.

Salad leaves can even be cooked. Baked Chicory with

Parma Ham is a famous classic, while Radicchio Pizza

gives a modern twist to an old favourite.

WATERCRESS SOUP

SERVES FOUR

INGREDIENTS

15ml/1 tbsp sunflower oil
15g/½oz/1 tbsp butter
1 onion, finely chopped
1 potato, diced
about 175g/6oz watercress or rocket
   (arugula)
400ml/14fl oz/1⅔ cups chicken
   or vegetable stock
400ml/14fl oz/1⅔ cups milk
lemon juice
salt and freshly ground black pepper
sour cream, to serve (optional)

1 Heat the oil and butter in a large pan and fry the onion over a gentle heat until soft but not browned. Add the potato, fry gently for 2–3 minutes and then cover and sweat for 5 minutes over a gentle heat, stirring occasionally.

2 Strip the watercress leaves from the stalks and roughly chop the stalks.

3 Add the stock and milk to the pan, stir in the chopped stalks and season with salt and pepper. Bring to the boil and then simmer gently, partially covered, for 10–12 minutes until the potatoes are tender. Add all but a few of the watercress leaves and simmer for 2 minutes.

4 Process the soup in a food processor or blender, and then pour into a clean pan and heat gently with the reserved watercress leaves. Taste when hot and add a little lemon juice and adjust the seasoning.

5 Pour the soup into warmed soup dishes and swirl in a little sour cream, if using, just before serving.

COOK'S TIP
Provided you leave out the cream, this is a low calorie but nutritious soup, which, served with crusty bread, makes a very satisfying meal.

WATERCRESS AND TWO-FISH TERRINE

THIS IS A PRETTY, DELICATE DISH, IDEAL FOR A SUMMER BUFFET PARTY OR PICNIC. SERVE WITH LEMON MAYONNAISE OR SOUR CREAM, AND A WATERCRESS AND GREEN SALAD.

SERVES SIX TO EIGHT

INGREDIENTS

350g/12oz monkfish, filleted
175g/6oz lemon sole, filleted
1 egg and 1 egg white
45–60ml/3–4 tbsp lemon juice
40–50g/1½–2oz/1 cup fresh white
   breadcrumbs
300ml/½ pint/1¼ cups whipping
   cream
75g/3oz smoked salmon
175g/6oz watercress or rocket
   (arugula), roughly chopped
salt and freshly ground black pepper

1 Preheat the oven to 180°C/350°F/Gas 4 and line a 1.5 litre/2½ pint/6¼ cup loaf pan with non-stick baking paper.

2 Cut the fish into chunks, discarding the skin and bones. Put the fish into a food processor with a little salt and pepper.

3 Process briefly and add the egg and egg white, lemon juice, breadcrumbs and cream. Process to a paste. Put the mixture into a bowl. Take 75ml/5 tbsp of the mixture and process with the smoked salmon. Transfer to a separate bowl. Take 75ml/5 tbsp of the white fish mixture and process with the watercress.

4 Spoon half of the white fish mixture into the base of the prepared loaf tin and smooth the surface with a metal spatula.

5 Spread over the watercress mixture, then the smoked salmon mixture and finally spread over the remaining white fish mixture and smooth the top.

6 Lay a piece of buttered non-stick baking paper on top of the mixture and then cover with foil. Place the loaf tin in a roasting pan, half-filled with boiling water and cook in the oven for 1¼–1½ hours. Towards the end of the cooking time the terrine will begin to rise, which indicates that it is ready.

7 Allow to cool in the tin and then turn on to a serving plate and peel away the baking paper. Chill for 1–2 hours.

RADICCHIO PIZZA

*THIS UNUSUAL PIZZA TOPPING CONSISTS OF CHOPPED RADICCHIO WITH LEEKS, TOMATOES AND
PARMESAN AND MOZZARELLA CHEESES. THE BASE IS A SCONE DOUGH, MAKING THIS A QUICK AND EASY
SUPPER DISH TO PREPARE. SERVE WITH A CRISP GREEN SALAD.*

SERVES TWO

INGREDIENTS
½ x 400g/14oz can chopped tomatoes
2 garlic cloves, crushed
a pinch of dried basil
25ml/1½ tbsp olive oil, plus extra
 for dipping
2 leeks, sliced
100g/3½oz radicchio, roughly
 chopped
20g/¾oz Parmesan cheese, grated
115g/4oz mozzarella cheese, sliced
10–12 black olives, pitted
basil leaves, to garnish
salt and freshly ground black pepper
For the dough
225g/8oz/2 cups self-raising (self-
 rising) flour
2.5ml/½ tsp salt
50g/2oz/¼ cup butter or margarine
about 120ml/4fl oz/½ cup milk

1 Preheat the oven to 220°C/425°F/
Gas 7 and grease a baking sheet. Mix the
flour and salt in a bowl, rub in the butter
or margarine and gradually stir in the
milk and mix to a soft dough.

2 Roll the dough out on a lightly floured
surface to make a 25–28cm/10–11in
round. Place on the baking sheet.

3 Purée the tomatoes and then pour
into a small pan. Stir in one of the
crushed garlic cloves, together with the
dried basil and seasoning, and simmer
over a moderate heat until the mixture is
thick and reduced by about half.

4 Heat the olive oil in a large frying pan
and fry the leeks and remaining garlic for
4–5 minutes until slightly softened. Add
the chopped radicchio and cook, stirring
continuously for a few minutes, and then
cover and simmer gently for about
5–10 minutes. Stir in the Parmesan
cheese and season with salt and pepper.

5 Cover the dough base with the tomato
mixture and then spoon the leek and
radicchio mixture on top. Arrange the
mozzarella slices on top and scatter over
the black olives. Dip a few basil leaves in
olive oil, arrange on top and then bake
the pizza for 15–20 minutes until the
scone base and top are golden brown.

WARM DUCK SALAD WITH ORANGE

THE DISTINCT, SHARP FLAVOUR OF RADICCHIO, CURLY ENDIVE AND FRESH ORANGES COMPLEMENTS THE RICH TASTE OF THE DUCK TO MAKE THIS A SUPERB DISH. IT IS GOOD SERVED WITH STEAMED BABY NEW POTATOES FOR AN ELEGANT MAIN COURSE.

SERVES FOUR

INGREDIENTS
    2 duck breast fillets
    salt
    2 oranges
    frisée lettuce, radicchio and lamb's
       lettuce
    30ml/2 tbsp medium dry sherry
    10–15ml/2–3 tsp dark soy sauce

1 Rub the skin of the duck fillets with salt and then slash the skin several times with a sharp knife.

2 Heat a heavy cast-iron frying pan and fry the duck fillets, skin side down at first, for 20–25 minutes, turning once, until the skin is well browned and the flesh is cooked to your preference. Transfer to a plate to cool slightly and pour off the excess fat from the pan.

3 Peel the oranges then separate into segments and use a knife to remove all the pith, catching the juice in a small bowl. Arrange the salad leaves in a shallow serving bowl.

4 Heat the duck juices in the pan and stir in 45ml/3 tbsp of the reserved orange juice. Bring to the boil, add the sherry and then just enough soy sauce to give a piquant, spicy flavour.

5 Cut the duck into thick slices and arrange over the salad. Pour over the warm dressing and serve.

BAKED CHICORY WITH PROSCIUTTO

ALTHOUGH CHICORY IS SOMETIMES TOO HARSHLY FLAVOURED FOR SOME PEOPLE'S TASTES, SIMMERING IT BEFORE BRAISING ELIMINATES ANY BITTERNESS SO THAT THE FLAVOUR IS PLEASANTLY MILD.

SERVES FOUR

INGREDIENTS
4 heads of chicory (Belgian endive)
25g/1oz/2 tbsp butter
250ml/8fl oz/1 cup vegetable
  or chicken stock
4 slices prosciutto
75g/3oz mascarpone cheese
50g/2oz Emmenthal or Cheddar
  cheese, sliced
salt and freshly ground black pepper

4 Remove the chicory using a slotted spoon. Lay out the prosciutto slices and place one piece of chicory on each of the slices. Roll up and place, side by side, in a single layer in the prepared dish.

5 Simmer the stock until it is reduced by about half and then remove from the heat. Stir in the mascarpone cheese and pour the sauce over the chicory. Lay the slices of Emmenthal or Cheddar cheese over the top and bake in the oven for about 15 minutes until the top is golden and the sauce is bubbling.

1 Preheat the oven to 180°C/350°F/Gas 4. Grease an ovenproof dish. Trim the chicory and remove the central core.

2 Melt the butter in a large pan and gently sauté the chicory over a moderate heat for 4–5 minutes, turning occasionally, until the outer leaves begin to turn transparent.

3 Add the stock and a little seasoning, bring to the boil and then cover and simmer gently for 5–6 minutes until the chicory is almost tender.

ROCKET AND GRILLED CHÈVRE SALAD

FOR THIS RECIPE, LOOK OUT FOR CYLINDER-SHAPED GOAT'S CHEESE FROM A DELICATESSEN OR FOR SMALL ROLLS THAT CAN BE CUT INTO HALVES, WEIGHING ABOUT 50G/2OZ. SERVE ONE PER PERSON AS A STARTER OR DOUBLE THE RECIPE AND SERVE TWO EACH FOR A LIGHT LUNCH.

SERVES FOUR

INGREDIENTS

about 15ml/1 tbsp olive oil
about 15ml/1 tbsp vegetable oil
4 slices French bread
45ml/3 tbsp walnut oil
15ml/1 tbsp lemon juice
225g/8oz cylinder-shaped goat's cheese
a handful of rocket (arugula) leaves
about 115g/4oz frisée lettuce
salt and freshly ground black pepper
For the sauce
45ml/3 tbsp apricot jam
60ml/4 tbsp white wine
5ml/2 tsp Dijon mustard

1 Heat the two oils in a frying pan and fry the slices of French bread on one side only, until lightly golden. Transfer to a plate lined with kitchen paper.

4 Preheat the grill (broiler) a few minutes before serving the salad. Cut the goat's cheese into 50g/2oz rounds and place each piece on a croûton, untoasted side up. Place under the grill and cook for 3–4 minutes until the cheese melts.

5 Toss the rocket and lettuce in the walnut oil dressing and arrange attractively on four individual serving plates. When the cheese croûtons are ready, arrange on each plate and pour over a little of the apricot sauce.

2 To make the sauce, heat the jam in a small pan until warm but not boiling. Push through a sieve (strainer), into a clean pan, to remove the pieces of fruit, and then stir in the white wine and mustard. Heat gently and keep warm until ready to serve.

3 Blend the walnut oil and lemon juice and season with a little salt and pepper.

CHINESE LEAVES AND MOOLI WITH SCALLOPS

HERE'S A SPEEDY STIR-FRY MADE USING CHINESE LEAVES, MOOLI AND SCALLOPS. BOTH THE MOOLI AND CHINESE LEAVES HAVE A PLEASANT CRUNCHY "BITE". YOU NEED TO WORK QUICKLY, SO HAVE EVERYTHING PREPARED BEFORE YOU START COOKING.

SERVES FOUR

INGREDIENTS
    10 prepared scallops
    75ml/5 tbsp vegetable oil
    3 garlic cloves, finely chopped
    1cm/½in piece fresh root ginger,
      finely sliced
    4–5 spring onions (scallions), cut
      lengthways into 2.5cm/1in pieces
    30ml/2 tbsp medium dry sherry
    ½ mooli (daikon), cut into
      1cm/½in slices
    1 head Chinese leaves (Chinese cabbage),
      chopped lengthways into thin strips
For the marinade
    5ml/1 tsp cornflour (cornstarch)
    1 egg white, lightly beaten
    a pinch of white pepper
For the sauce
    5ml/1 tsp cornflour (cornstarch)
    45ml/3 tbsp oyster sauce

6 Heat another 30ml/2 tbsp of oil in the wok, add the remaining garlic, ginger and spring onions and then stir-fry for 1 minute. Add the corals, stir-fry briefly and transfer to a dish.

1 Rinse the scallops and separate the corals from the white meat. Cut each scallop into 2–3 pieces and slice the corals. Place them on two dishes.

2 For the marinade, blend together the cornflour, egg white and white pepper. Pour half over the scallops and the rest over the corals. Leave for 10 minutes.

3 To make the sauce, blend the cornflour with 60ml/4 tbsp water and the oyster sauce and set aside.

4 Heat about 30ml/2 tbsp of the oil in a wok, add half of the garlic and let it sizzle, and then add half the ginger and half of the spring onions. Stir-fry for about 30 seconds and then stir in the scallops (not the corals).

5 Stir-fry for 30–60 seconds until the scallops start to become opaque, then reduce the heat and add 15ml/1 tbsp of the sherry. Cook briefly and then spoon the scallops and the cooking liquid into a bowl and set aside.

7 Heat the remaining oil and add the mooli. Stir-fry for about 30 seconds and then stir in the cabbage. Stir-fry for about 30 seconds more then add the oyster sauce mixture and about 60ml/4 tbsp water. Allow the cabbage to simmer briefly and then stir in the scallops and corals, together with all their liquid, and cook briefly to heat through.

RADISH, MANGO AND APPLE SALAD

RADISH IS A YEAR-ROUND VEGETABLE AND THIS SALAD CAN BE SERVED AT ANY TIME OF YEAR, WITH ITS CLEAN, CRISP TASTES AND MELLOW FLAVOURS. SERVE WITH SMOKED FISH, SUCH AS ROLLS OF SMOKED SALMON, OR WITH CONTINENTAL HAM OR SALAMI.

SERVES FOUR

INGREDIENTS

    10–15 radishes
    1 apple, peeled cored and
     thinly sliced
    2 celery sticks, thinly sliced
    1 small ripe mango
    salt and freshly ground black pepper
    sprigs of dill, to garnish
For the dressing
    120ml/4fl oz/½ cup sour cream
    10ml/2 tsp creamed horseradish
    15ml/1 tbsp chopped fresh dill

3 Cut through the mango lengthways either side of the stone (pit) and make even criss-cross cuts through each side section. Bend each section back to separate the cubes, remove them with a small knife and add to the bowl. Pour the dressing over the vegetables and fruit and stir gently so that all the ingredients are coated in the dressing. When ready to serve, spoon the salad into an attractive salad bowl and garnish with sprigs of dill.

1 To prepare the dressing, blend together the sour cream, horseradish and dill in a small jug or bowl and season with a little salt and pepper.

2 Top and tail the radishes and then slice them thinly. Add to a bowl together with the thinly sliced apple and celery.

CHICKEN LIVERS AND GREEN SALAD

CHICKEN LIVERS HAVE A WONDERFULLY ROBUST FLAVOUR THAT COMPLEMENTS A SALAD WITH A PIQUANT DRESSING. IF YOU ARE SHORT OF TIME YOU CAN BUY READY PREPARED SALADS WHICH ARE AVAILABLE FROM MOST SUPERMARKETS.

SERVES FOUR

INGREDIENTS
a selection of fresh salad leaves
4 spring onions (scallions), finely
   sliced
15ml/1 tbsp roughly chopped
   flat leaf parsley
115g/4oz unsmoked streaky (fatty)
   bacon, chopped
450g/1lb chicken livers
seasoned plain (all-purpose) flour, for
   dusting
15ml/1 tbsp sunflower oil
25g/1oz/2 tbsp butter or margarine
salt and freshly ground black pepper
For the dressing
100ml/3½fl oz/⅓ cup sunflower oil
30–45ml/2–3 tbsp lemon juice
5ml/1 tsp French mustard
1 small garlic clove, crushed

1 To make the dressing, place the oil, lemon juice, French mustard, garlic and seasoning in a screw-top jar and shake vigorously to mix.

2 Place the salad leaves in a large bowl with the spring onions and parsley. Pour over the dressing, toss briefly and then arrange on four individual serving plates.

3 Dry-fry the bacon in a frying pan until golden brown. Transfer to a plate using a slotted spoon and keep warm.

4 Trim the chicken livers, pat dry on kitchen paper and then dust them thoroughly with the seasoned flour.

5 Heat the oil and butter or margarine in a frying pan; fry the livers over a fairly high heat for about 8 minutes, turning occasionally until cooked as preferred; either cooked through or slightly pink inside.

6 Arrange the chicken livers on the salad leaves and scatter the crisp bacon pieces over the top.

CAESAR SALAD

A CLASSIC SALAD WITH AN EGG YOLK DRESSING, THIS MUST BE MADE USING COS LETTUCE. THE ORIGINS OF ITS NAME ARE A MYSTERY. SOME PEOPLE SAY IT WAS INVENTED BY AN ITALIAN, CAESAR CARDINI, IN MEXICO, AND OTHERS CLAIM THAT IT COMES FROM CALIFORNIA.

SERVES FOUR

INGREDIENTS
1 cos or romaine lettuce
8 anchovies, chopped
40g/1½oz shavings of Parmesan
   cheese
For the dressing
2 egg yolks
2.5ml/½ tsp French mustard
50ml/2fl oz/¼ cup olive oil
50ml/2fl oz/¼ cup sunflower oil
15ml/1 tbsp white wine vinegar
a pinch of salt
For the croûtons
1 garlic clove, crushed
60–75ml/4–5 tbsp olive oil
75g/3oz stale white bread,
   cut into cubes

1 Place the garlic in the oil and set aside for about 30 minutes for the garlic flavour to infuse into the oil.

2 To make the dressing, place the egg yolks, mustard, olive oil, sunflower oil, vinegar and salt in a screw-top jar and shake well to emulsify.

3 To make the croûtons, strain the garlic oil into a frying pan and discard the garlic. When hot, fry the bread until golden and then drain on kitchen paper.

4 Arrange the lettuce leaves in a salad bowl. Pour over the dressing and gently fold in the anchovies and croûtons. Scatter with Parmesan shavings.

APPLES, PEARS AND STONE FRUITS

Apples, pears and stone fruits (those with pits) are
wonderfully versatile. Fresh Cherry Hazelnut
Strudel and Pear and Cinnamon Fritters are just two
of the tempting tea-time treats in store, while Plum
and Custard Creams and Apple Crêpes with
Butterscotch Sauce make memorable desserts. Stone
fruits are often grown in greenhouses, but nothing
beats the taste of a sun-ripened fruit, so it is worth
waiting until they are in season.

APPLE CRÊPES WITH BUTTERSCOTCH SAUCE

THESE WONDERFUL DESSERT CRÊPES ARE FLAVOURED WITH SWEET CIDER, FILLED WITH CARAMELIZED APPLES AND DRIZZLED WITH A RICH, SMOOTH BUTTERSCOTCH SAUCE.

3 Make the filling. Core the apples and cut them into thick slices. Heat 15g/ ½ oz/1 tbsp of the butter in a large frying pan. Add the apples to the pan. Cook until golden on both sides, then transfer the slices to a bowl with a slotted spoon and set them aside.

4 Add the rest of the butter to the pan. As soon as it has melted, add the muscovado sugar. When the sugar has dissolved and the mixture is bubbling, stir in the cream. Continue cooking until it forms a smooth sauce.

5 Fold each pancake in half, then fold in half again to form a cone; fill each with some of the fried apples. Place two filled pancakes on each dessert plate, drizzle over some of the butterscotch sauce and serve at once.

SERVES FOUR

INGREDIENTS
    115g/4oz/1 cup plain (all-purpose) flour
    a pinch of salt
    2 eggs
    175ml/6fl oz/¾ cup creamy milk
    120ml/4fl oz/½ cup sweet cider
    butter, for frying
For the filling and sauce
    4 Braeburn apples
    90g/3½ oz/scant ½ cup butter
    225g/8oz/1⅓ cups light muscovado
      (brown) sugar
    150ml/¼ pint/⅔ cup double (heavy)
      cream

1 Make the crêpe batter. Sift the flour and salt into a large bowl. Add the eggs and milk and beat until smooth. Stir in the cider; set aside for 30 minutes.

2 Heat a small heavy non-stick frying pan. Add a knob (pat) of butter and ladle in enough batter to coat the base of the pan thinly. Cook until the crêpe is golden underneath, then flip it over and cook the other side until it is golden. Slide the crêpe on to a plate. Repeat the process with the remaining mixture to make seven more.

VARIATIONS
You could just as easily use plums, pears, strawberries or bananas to fill the crêpes. If you like, add a touch of Grand Marnier to the apples towards the end of cooking.

PEAR AND CINNAMON FRITTERS

IF YOU DON'T LIKE DEEP FRYING AS A RULE, DO MAKE AN EXCEPTION FOR THIS DISH. FRITTERS ARE IRRESISTIBLE, AND A WONDERFUL WAY OF PERSUADING CHILDREN TO EAT MORE FRUIT.

SERVES FOUR

INGREDIENTS
3 ripe, firm pears
30ml/2 tbsp caster (superfine) sugar
30ml/2 tbsp Kirsch
groundnut (peanut) oil, for frying
50g/2oz/1 cup amaretti, finely crushed
For the batter
75g/3oz/¾ cup plain (all-purpose)
    flour
1.5ml/¼ tsp salt
1.5ml/¼ tsp ground cinnamon
60ml/4 tbsp milk
2 eggs, separated
45ml/3 tbsp water
To serve
30ml/2 tbsp caster (superfine) sugar
1.5ml/¼ tsp ground cinnamon
clotted cream

1 Peel the pears, cut them in quarters and remove the cores. Toss the wedges in the caster sugar and Kirsch. Set aside for 15 minutes.

2 Make the batter. Sift the flour, salt and cinnamon into a large bowl. Beat in the milk, egg yolks and water until smooth. Set aside for 10 minutes.

3 Whisk the egg whites in a grease-free bowl until they form stiff peaks; lightly fold them into the batter. Preheat the oven to 150°C/300°F/Gas 2.

4 Pour oil into a deep heavy pan to a depth of 7.5cm/3in. Heat to 185°C/360°F or until a bread cube, added to the oil, browns in 45 seconds.

5 Toss a pear wedge in the amaretti crumbs, then spear it on a fork and dip it into the batter until evenly coated. Lower it gently into the hot oil and use a knife to push it off the fork. Add more wedges in the same way but do not overcrowd the pan. Cook the fritters for 3–4 minutes or until golden. Drain on kitchen paper. Keep hot in the oven while cooking successive batches.

6 Mix the sugar and cinnamon and sprinkle some over the fritters. Sprinkle a little cinnamon sugar over the clotted cream; serve with the hot fritters.

VARIATIONS
Also try apples, apricots and bananas.

POACHED PEARS IN PORT SYRUP

THE PERFECT CHOICE FOR AUTUMN ENTERTAINING, THIS SIMPLE DESSERT HAS A BEAUTIFUL RICH COLOUR AND FANTASTIC FLAVOUR THANKS TO THE TASTES OF PORT AND LEMON.

SERVES FOUR

INGREDIENTS

2 ripe, firm pears, such as Williams
  or Comice
pared rind of 1 lemon
175ml/6fl oz/¾ cup ruby port
50g/2oz/¼ cup caster (supefine) sugar
1 cinnamon stick
60ml/4 tbsp cold water
fresh cream, to serve
To decorate
  30ml/2 tbsp sliced hazelnuts, toasted
  fresh mint, pear or rose leaves

COOK'S TIP
Choose pears of similar size, with the stalks intact, for the most attractive effect when fanned on the plate.

1 Peel the pears, cut them in half and remove the cores. Place the lemon rind, port, sugar, cinnamon stick and water in a shallow pan. Bring to the boil over a low heat. Add the pears, lower the heat, cover and poach for 5 minutes. Let the pears cool in the syrup.

2 When the pears are cold, transfer them to a bowl with a slotted spoon. Return the syrup to the heat. Boil rapidly until it has reduced to form a syrup that will coat the back of a spoon lightly. Remove the cinnamon stick and lemon rind and leave the syrup to cool.

3 To serve, place each pear in turn on a board, cut side down. Keeping it intact at the stalk end, slice it lengthways, then using a metal spatula, carefully lift it off and place on a dessert plate. Press gently so that the pear fans out. When all the pears have been fanned, spoon over the port syrup. Top each portion with a few hazelnuts and decorate with fresh mint, pear or rose leaves. Serve with cream.

APPLE CHARLOTTES

THESE TEMPTING LITTLE FRUIT CHARLOTTES ARE A WONDERFUL WAY TO USE WINDFALLS.

SERVES FOUR

INGREDIENTS

175g/6oz/¾ cup butter
450g/1lb Bramley apples
225g/8oz Braeburn apples
60ml/4 tbsp water
130g/4½oz/scant ⅔ cup caster
  (superfine) sugar
2 egg yolks
a pinch of grated nutmeg
9 thin slices white bread, crusts
  removed
extra-thick double (heavy) cream or
  custard, to serve

COOK'S TIP

A mixture of cooking and eating apples
gives the best flavour, but you can use
cooking apples; just sweeten to taste.

1 Preheat the oven to 190°C/375°F/
Gas 5. Put a knob (pat) of the butter in
a pan. Peel and core the apples, dice
them finely and put them in the pan
with the water. Cover and cook for 10
minutes or until the cooking apples
have pulped down. Stir in 115g/4oz/
½ cup of the caster sugar. Then boil,
uncovered, until any liquid has
evaporated and what remains is a thick
pulp. Remove from the heat, beat in the
egg yolks and nutmeg and set aside.

2 Melt the remaining butter in a
separate pan over a low heat until the
white curds start to separate from the
clear yellow liquid. Remove from the
heat. Leave to stand for a few minutes,
then strain the clear clarified butter
through a muslin-lined sieve.

3 Brush four 150ml/¼ pint/⅔ cup
individual charlotte moulds or pudding
tins with a little of the clarified butter;
sprinkle with the remaining caster
sugar. Cut the bread slices into
2.5cm/1in strips. Dip the strips into
the remaining clarified butter; use to
line the moulds or tins. Overlap the
strips on the base to give the effect of a
swirl and let the excess bread overhang
the tops of the moulds or tins.

4 Fill each bread case with apple pulp.
Fold the excess bread over the top of
each mould or tin to make a lid; press
down lightly. Bake for 45–50 minutes or
until golden. Run a knife between each
charlotte and its mould or tin, then turn
out on to dessert plates. Serve with
extra-thick double cream or custard.

SPICED APPLE CRUMBLE

ANY FRUIT CAN BE USED IN THIS POPULAR DESSERT, BUT YOU CAN'T BEAT THE FAVOURITES OF
BLACKBERRY AND APPLE. HAZELNUTS AND CARDAMOM SEEDS GIVE THE TOPPING EXTRA FLAVOUR.

SERVES FOUR TO SIX

INGREDIENTS
    butter, for greasing
    450g/1lb Bramley apples
    115g/4oz/1 cup blackberries
    grated rind and juice of 1 orange
    50g/2oz/⅓ cup light muscovado
      (brown) sugar
    custard, to serve
For the topping
    175g/6oz/1½ cups plain (all-purpose)
      flour
    75g/3oz/⅓ cup butter
    75g/3oz/⅓ cup caster sugar
    25g/1oz/¼ cup chopped hazelnuts
    2.5ml/½ tsp crushed cardamom seeds

VARIATIONS
This dessert can be made with all sorts of
fruit. Try plums, peaches or pears, alone or
with apples. Rhubarb makes a delectable
crumble, especially with bananas.

1 Preheat the oven to 200°C/400°F/
Gas 6. Generously butter a 1.2 litre/
2 pint/5 cup baking dish. Peel and
core the apples, then slice them into
the prepared baking dish. Level the
surface, then scatter the blackberries
over. Sprinkle the orange rind and light
muscovado sugar evenly over the top,
then pour over the orange juice. Set the
fruit mixture aside while you make the
crumble topping.

2 Make the topping. Sift the flour into a
bowl and rub in the butter until the
mixture resembles coarse breadcrumbs.
Stir in the caster sugar, hazelnuts and
cardamom seeds. Scatter the topping
over the top of the fruit.

3 Press the topping around the edges
of the dish to seal in the juices. Bake
for 30–35 minutes or until the crumble
is golden. Serve hot, with custard.

BAKED STUFFED APPLES

THIS TRADITIONAL APPLE DESSERT IS EXCEPTIONALLY SIMPLE TO MAKE. BAKE THE APPLES IN THE OVEN
ON THE SHELF UNDER THE SUNDAY ROAST FOR A DELICIOUS END TO THE MEAL.

SERVES FOUR

INGREDIENTS
    4 large Bramley apples
    75g/3oz/½ cup light muscovado
      (brown) sugar
    75g/3oz/⅓ cup butter, softened
    grated rind and juice of ½ orange
    1.5ml/¼ tsp ground cinnamon
    30ml/2 tbsp crushed ratafia biscuits
      (almond macaroons)
    50g/2oz/½ cup pecan nuts, chopped
    50g/2oz/½ cup luxury mixed glacé
      (candied) fruit, chopped

COOK'S TIP
Use a little butter or oil to grease the
baking dish, if you like, or pour a small
amount of water around the stuffed
apples to stop them sticking to the dish.

1 Preheat the oven to 180°C/350°F/
Gas 4. Wash and dry the apples.
Remove the cores with an apple corer,
then carefully enlarge each core cavity
to twice its size, by shaving off more
flesh with the corer. Score each apple
around its equator, using a sharp knife.
Stand the apples in a baking dish.

2 Mix the sugar, butter, orange rind
and juice, cinnamon and ratafia crumbs.
Beat well, then stir in the nuts and
glacé fruit. Divide the filling among the
apples, piling it high. Shield the filling in
each apple with a small piece of foil.
Bake for 45–60 minutes until all the
apples are tender.

PLUM AND CUSTARD CREAMS

IF YOU WERE RELUCTANTLY RAISED ON STEWED PLUMS AND CUSTARD, THIS SOPHISTICATED VERSION, PRETTILY LAYERED IN A GLASS, WILL BRING A SMILE TO YOUR LIPS.

SERVES SIX

INGREDIENTS

675g/1½lb red plums, stoned (pitted) and sliced
grated rind and juice of 1 orange
50g/2oz/¼ cup caster (superfine) sugar
400g/14oz carton ready-made custard
300ml/½ pint/1¼ cups double (heavy) cream
30ml/2 tbsp water
15ml/1 tbsp powdered gelatine
1 egg white
plum slices and fresh mint sprigs, to decorate

1 Put the plums in a pan with the orange rind and juice. Add the caster sugar and heat, stirring constantly, until the sugar has dissolved. Cook the plums for 5 minutes until tender. Cool slightly, then purée in a food processor until smooth. Press through a sieve into a bowl and set aside to cool.

2 Put the custard in a pan, add half the cream and heat until boiling. Meanwhile, pour the water into a heatproof bowl and sprinkle the gelatine on top; set aside for 5 minutes until sponged. Whisk the soaked gelatine into the hot custard until it has dissolved. Allow the mixture to cool.

3 Whip the remaining cream to soft peaks, then fold it into the custard mixture. In a grease-free bowl, whisk the egg white to soft peaks; fold it into the custard too. Set aside, stirring occasionally, until just starting to set.

4 Quickly spoon alternate spoonfuls of the custard and plum purée into six tall dessert glasses. Use a long metal skewer or thin metal spoon handle to marble the mixtures together. Chill for 2–3 hours or until the custard has set. Decorate each dessert with plum slices and fresh mint sprigs just before serving.

SPICED FRUITS JUBILEE

BASED ON THE CLASSIC CHERRIES JUBILEE, THIS IS A GREAT WAY TO USE A GLUT OF ANY STONE FRUIT. THE SPICED SYRUP IS A DELICIOUS BONUS. SERVE WITH THE BEST DAIRY VANILLA ICE CREAM.

SERVES SIX

INGREDIENTS
115g/4oz/½ cup caster (superfine) sugar
thinly pared rind of 1 unwaxed lemon
1 cinnamon stick
4 whole cloves
300ml/½ pint/1¼ cups water
225g/8oz tart red plums, pitted and sliced
225g/8oz nectarines, stoned (pitted) and chopped
225g/8oz/1½ cups cherries, stoned (pitted)
5ml/1 tsp arrowroot
75ml/5 tbsp brandy
vanilla ice cream, to serve

1 Put the sugar, lemon rind, cinnamon stick, cloves and water in a pan. Bring to the boil, stirring. Lower the heat and simmer for 5 minutes, then lift out the spices with a slotted spoon and discard.

2 Add the fruit, cover the pan and simmer for 5 minutes. Drain the fruit and set it aside; return the syrup to the pan. Boil it, uncovered, for 2 minutes or until thick and syrupy.

3 Put the arrowroot in a small bowl and stir in 30ml/2 tbsp of the brandy. Stir the mixture into the syrup. Continue cooking and stirring, until the sauce thickens. Return the fruit to the pan.

4 Place scoops of ice cream in serving bowls and spoon the hot fruit over. Warm the remaining brandy in a small pan, then set it alight. Ladle it over the fruit at the table for maximum effect.

PEACH MELBA SYLLABUB

IF YOU ARE MAKING THESE SOPHISTICATED TEMPTATIONS FOR A DINNER PARTY, COOK THE PEACHES AND RASPBERRIES THE DAY BEFORE TO ALLOW THE FRUIT TO CHILL. WHIP UP THE SYLLABUB AT THE VERY LAST MINUTE TO MAKE A DELICIOUS, LIGHT-AS-A-CLOUD TOPPING.

SERVES SIX

INGREDIENTS
    4 peaches, peeled and sliced
    300ml/½ pint/1¼ cups blush or red
      grape juice
    115g/4oz/⅔ cup raspberries
    raspberry or mint leaves, to decorate
    ratafias (almond macaroons) or other
      dessert biscuits (cookies), to serve
For the syllabub
    60ml/4 tbsp peach schnapps
    30ml/2 tbsp blush or red grape juice
    300ml/½ pint/1¼ cups double
      (heavy) cream

VARIATIONS
Use dessert pears and sliced kiwi fruit.
Instead of the syllabub, top the fruit with
whipped cream flavoured with Advocaat
and finely chopped stem ginger.

1 Place the peach slices in a large pan.
Add the grape juice. Bring to the boil,
then cover, lower the heat and simmer
for 5–7 minutes or until tender.

2 Add the raspberries and remove from
the heat. Set aside in the refrigerator
until cold. Divide the peach and raspberry
mixture among six dessert glasses.

3 For the syllabub, place the peach
schnapps and grape juice in a large
bowl and whisk in the cream until it
forms soft peaks.

4 Spoon the syllabub on top of the fruit
and decorate each portion with a fresh
raspberry or mint leaf. Serve with
ratafias or other dessert biscuits.

NECTARINE AND HAZELNUT MERINGUES

IF IT'S INDULGENCE YOU'RE SEEKING, LOOK NO FURTHER. SWEET NECTARINES AND CREAM SYLLABUB PAIRED WITH CRISP HAZELNUT MERINGUES MAKE A SUPERB SWEET.

SERVES FIVE

INGREDIENTS
    3 egg whites
    175g/6oz/¾ cup caster (superfine)
      sugar
    50g/2oz/½ cup chopped
      hazelnuts, toasted
    300ml/½ pint/1¼ cups double
      (heavy) cream
    60ml/4 tbsp sweet dessert wine
    2 nectarines, stoned (pitted) and
      sliced
    fresh mint sprigs, to decorate

VARIATIONS
Use apricots instead of nectarines if you
prefer, or try this with a raspberry filling.

1 Preheat the oven to 140°C/275°F/
Gas 1. Line two large baking sheets with
non-stick baking paper. Whisk or beat
the egg whites in a grease-free bowl
until they form stiff peaks when the
whisk or beaters are lifted. Gradually
whisk in the caster sugar a spoonful at
a time until the mixture forms a stiff,
glossy meringue.

2 Fold in two-thirds of the chopped
toasted hazelnuts, then spoon five large
ovals on to each lined baking sheet.
Scatter the remaining hazelnuts over
five of the meringue ovals. Flatten the
tops of the remaining five ovals.

3 Bake the meringues for 1–1¼ hours
until crisp and dry, then carefully lift
them off the baking paper and cool
completely on a wire rack.

4 Whip the cream with the dessert
wine until the mixture forms soft peaks.
Spoon some of the cream syllabub on to
each of the plain meringues. Arrange a
few nectarine slices on each. Put each
meringue on a dessert plate with a
hazelnut-topped meringue. Decorate
each portion with mint sprigs and serve
the meringues immediately.

CARAMELIZED APRICOTS WITH PAIN PERDU

PAIN PERDU IS A FRENCH INVENTION THAT LITERALLY TRANSLATES AS "LOST BREAD". AMERICANS CALL IT FRENCH TOAST, WHILE A BRITISH VERSION IS KNOWN AS POOR KNIGHTS OF WINDSOR.

SERVES FOUR

INGREDIENTS
    75g/3oz/6 tbsp unsalted (sweet)
      butter, clarified
    450g/1lb apricots, stoned (pitted)
      and thickly sliced
    115g/4oz/½ cup caster (superfine)
      sugar
    150ml/¼ pint/⅔ cup double (heavy)
      cream
    30ml/2 tbsp apricot brandy or brandy
For the pain perdu
    600ml/1 pint/2½ cups milk
    1 vanilla pod (bean)
    50g/2oz/¼ cup caster (superfine)
      sugar
    4 large (US extra large) eggs, beaten
    115g/4oz/½ cup unsalted (sweet)
      butter, clarified
    6 brioche slices, diagonally halved
    2.5ml/½ tsp ground cinnamon

1 Heat a heavy frying pan, then melt a quarter of the butter. Add the apricot slices and cook for 2–3 minutes until golden. Using a slotted spoon, transfer them to a bowl. Add the rest of the butter to the pan with the sugar and heat gently, stirring, until golden.

2 Pour in the cream and apricot or brandy and cook gently until the mixture forms a smooth sauce. Boil for 2–3 minutes until thickened, pour the sauce over the apricots and set aside.

3 To make the pain perdu, pour the milk into a pan and add the vanilla pod and half the sugar. Heat gently until almost boiling, then set aside to cool.

4 Remove the vanilla pod and pour the flavoured milk into a shallow dish. Whisk in the eggs. Heat a sixth of the butter in the clean frying pan. Dip each slice of brioche in turn into the milk mixture, add it to the pan and fry until golden brown on both sides. Add the remaining butter as needed. As the pain perdu is cooked, remove the slices; keep hot.

5 Warm the apricot sauce and spoon it on to the pain perdu. Mix the remaining sugar with the cinnamon and sprinkle a little of the mixture over each portion.

COOK'S TIP
To clarify the butter, melt it in a small pan, then leave it to stand for a few minutes. Carefully pour the clear butter (the clarified butter) on the surface into a small bowl, leaving the milky solids behind in the pan.

FRESH CHERRY AND HAZELNUT STRUDEL

SERVE THIS WONDERFUL OLD-WORLD TREAT AS A WARM DESSERT WITH CUSTARD, OR ALLOW IT TO COOL AND OFFER IT AS A SCRUMPTIOUS CAKE WITH AFTERNOON TEA OR COFFEE.

SERVES SIX TO EIGHT

INGREDIENTS
    75g/3oz/6 tbsp butter
    90ml/6 tbsp light muscovado (brown)
      sugar
    3 egg yolks
    grated rind of 1 lemon
    1.5ml/¼ tsp grated nutmeg
    250g/9oz/generous 1 cup ricotta cheese
    8 large sheets filo pastry, thawed
      if frozen
    75g/3oz ratafias (almond macaroons),
      crushed
    450g/1lb/2½ cups cherries, pitted
    30ml/2 tbsp chopped hazelnuts
    icing (confectioners') sugar, for dusting
    crème fraîche, to serve

1 Preheat the oven to 190°C/375°F/ Gas 5. Soften 15g/½oz/1 tbsp of the butter. Place it in a bowl and beat in the sugar and egg yolks until light and fluffy. Beat in the lemon rind, nutmeg and ricotta, then set aside.

2 Melt the remaining butter in a small pan. Working quickly, place a sheet of filo on a clean dish towel and brush it generously with melted butter. Place a second sheet on top and repeat the process. Continue until all the filo has been layered and buttered, reserving some of the melted butter.

3 Scatter the crushed ratafias over the top, leaving a 5cm/2in border around the outside. Spoon the ricotta mixture over the biscuits, spread it lightly to cover, then scatter over the cherries.

4 Fold in the filo pastry border and use the dish towel to carefully roll up the strudel, Swiss-roll (jelly-roll) style, beginning from one of the long sides of the pastry. Grease a baking sheet with the remaining melted butter.

5 Place the strudel on the baking sheet and scatter the hazelnuts over the surface. Bake for 35–40 minutes or until the strudel is golden and crisp. Dust with icing sugar and serve with a dollop of crème fraîche.

BERRIES AND CITRUS FRUITS

For sheer beauty, berries take a lot of beating.
Make the most of their tantalizing colours and
flavours by serving them simply, as a topping for
ice cream or in a summer pudding. Citrus fruits
are wonderfully versatile; they can be juiced,
enjoyed just as they are or used in both sweet and
savoury dishes. Citrus Fruit Flambé with Pistachio
Praline and Summer Berry Crêpes are just some
of the delights to try.

FRESH BERRY PAVLOVA

*PAVLOVA IS THE SIMPLEST OF DESSERTS, BUT IT CAN ALSO BE THE MOST STUNNING. FILL WITH A MIX
OF BERRY FRUITS IF YOU LIKE — RASPBERRIES AND BLUEBERRIES MAKE A MARVELLOUS COMBINATION.*

SERVES SIX TO EIGHT

INGREDIENTS

4 egg whites, at room temperature
225g/8oz/1 cup caster (superfine) sugar
5ml/1 tsp cornflour (cornstarch)
5ml/1 tsp cider vinegar
2.5ml/½ tsp vanilla essence (extract)
300ml/½ pint/1¼ cups double
  (heavy) cream
150ml/¼ pint/⅔ cup crème fraîche
175g/6oz/1 cup raspberries
175g/6oz/1½ cups blueberries
fresh mint sprigs, to decorate
icing (confectioners') sugar, for dusting

COOK'S TIP
To begin, invert a plate on the baking
parchment and draw round it with a
pencil. Turn over and use the circle as a
guide for the meringue.

1 Preheat the oven to 140°C/275°F/
Gas 1. Line a baking sheet with baking
parchment. Whisk the egg whites in a
large grease-free bowl until they form
stiff peaks. Gradually whisk in the sugar
to make a stiff, glossy meringue. Sift the
cornflour over and fold it in with the
vinegar and vanilla.

2 Spoon the meringue mixture on to
the paper-lined sheet, using the circle
drawn on the paper as a guide (see
Cook's Tip). Spread into a round,
swirling the top, and bake for 1¼ hours
or until the meringue is crisp and very
lightly golden. Switch off the oven,
keeping the door closed, and allow the
meringue to cool for 1–2 hours.

3 Carefully peel the parchment from
the meringue and transfer it to a serving
plate. Whip the cream in a large mixing
bowl until it forms soft peaks, fold in the
crème fraîche, then spoon the mixture
into the centre of the meringue case.
Top with the raspberries and blueberries
and decorate with the fresh mint sprigs.
Sift icing sugar over the top of the
pavlova and serve immediately.

GOOSEBERRY AND ELDERFLOWER FOOL

GOOSEBERRIES AND ELDERFLOWERS ARE A MATCH MADE IN HEAVEN, EACH BRINGING OUT THE FLAVOUR OF THE OTHER. SERVE WITH AMARETTI OR OTHER DESSERT BISCUITS FOR DIPPING.

SERVES SIX

INGREDIENTS
    450g/1lb/4 cups gooseberries, trimmed
    30ml/2 tbsp water
    50–75g/2–3oz/¼–⅓ cup caster
      (superfine) sugar
    30ml/2 tbsp elderflower cordial
    400g/14oz carton ready-made custard
    green food colouring (optional)
    300ml/½ pint/1¼ cups double (heavy)
      cream
    crushed amaretti, to decorate
    amaretti, to serve

1 Put the gooseberries and water in a pan. Cover and cook for 5–6 minutes or until the berries pop open.

2 Add the sugar and elderflower cordial to the gooseberries, then stir vigorously or mash until the fruit forms a pulp. Remove the pan from the heat, spoon the gooseberry pulp into a bowl and set aside to cool.

3 Stir the custard into the fruit. Add a few drops of food colouring, if using. Whip the cream to soft peaks, then fold it into the mixture and chill. Serve in dessert glasses, decorated with crushed amaretti, and accompanied by amaretti.

FRUITS OF THE FOREST WITH WHITE CHOCOLATE CREAMS

COLOURFUL FRUITS MACERATED IN A MIXTURE OF WHITE COCONUT RUM AND SUGAR MAKE A FANTASTIC ACCOMPANIMENT TO A DELIGHTFULLY CREAMY WHITE CHOCOLATE MOUSSE.

SERVES FOUR

INGREDIENTS
- 75g/3oz white cooking (unsweetened) chocolate, in squares
- 150ml/¼ pint/⅔ cup double (heavy) cream
- 30ml/2 tbsp crème fraîche
- 1 egg, separated
- 5ml/1 tsp powdered gelatine
- 30ml/2 tbsp cold water
- a few drops of vanilla essence (extract)
- 115g/4oz/1 cup small strawberries, sliced
- 75g/3oz/½ cup raspberries
- 75g/3oz/¾ cup blueberries
- 45ml/3 tbsp caster (superfine) sugar
- 75ml/5 tbsp white coconut rum
- strawberry leaves, to decorate

1 Melt the chocolate in a heatproof bowl set over a pan of hot water. Heat the cream in a separate pan until almost boiling, then stir into the chocolate with the crème fraîche. Cool slightly, then beat in the egg yolk.

2 Sprinkle the gelatine over the cold water in another heatproof bowl and set aside for a few minutes to swell.

COOK'S TIP
For a dramatic effect, decorate each white chocolate cream with dark chocolate leaves, made by coating the veined side of unsprayed rose leaves with melted chocolate. Let it dry before gently pulling off the leaves.

3 Set the bowl in a pan of hot water until the gelatine has dissolved completely. Stir the dissolved gelatine into the chocolate mixture and add the vanilla essence. Set aside until starting to thicken and set.

4 Brush four dariole moulds or individual soufflé dishes with oil; line the base of each with baking parchment.

5 In a grease-free bowl, whisk the egg white to soft peaks, then fold into the chocolate mixture.

6 Spoon the mixture into the prepared dariole moulds or soufflé dishes, then level the surface of each and chill for 2–3 hours or until firm.

7 Meanwhile, place the fruits in a bowl. Add the caster sugar and coconut rum and stir gently to mix. Cover and chill until required.

8 Ease the chocolate cream away from the rims of the moulds or dishes and turn out on to dessert plates. Spoon the fruits around the outside. Decorate with the strawberry leaves, if using, then serve at once.

SUMMER BERRY CRÊPES

THE DELICATE FLAVOUR OF THESE FLUFFY CRÊPES CONTRASTS BEAUTIFULLY WITH TANGY BERRY FRUITS.

SERVES FOUR

INGREDIENTS
115g/4oz/1 cup self-raising (self-rising) flour
1 large (US extra large) egg
300ml/½ pint/1¼ cups milk
a few drops of vanilla essence (extract)
15g/½oz/1 tbsp butter
15ml/1 tbsp sunflower oil
icing (confectioners') sugar, for dusting
For the fruit
25g/1oz/2 tbsp butter
50g/2oz/¼ cup caster (superfine) sugar
thinly pared rind of ½ orange
juice of 2 oranges
350g/12oz/3 cups mixed summer berries, such as sliced strawberries, yellow raspberries, blueberries and redcurrants
45ml/3 tbsp Grand Marnier or other orange liqueur

1 Preheat the oven to 150°C/300°F/Gas 2. To make the crêpes, sift the flour into a large bowl and make a well in the centre. Break in the egg and gradually whisk in the milk to make a smooth batter. Stir in the vanilla essence. Set the batter aside in a cool place for up to half an hour.

2 Heat the butter and oil together in an 18cm/7in non-stick frying pan. Swirl to grease the pan, then pour off the excess fat into a small bowl.

3 If the batter has been allowed to stand, whisk it thoroughly until smooth. Pour a little of the batter into the hot pan, swirling to cover the base of the pan evenly. Cook until the mixture comes away from the sides and the crêpe is golden underneath.

4 Flip the crêpe over with a large palette knife and cook the other side briefly until golden.

5 Slide the crêpe on to a heatproof plate. Make seven more crêpes in the same way, greasing the pan with more butter and oil mixture as needed. Cover the crêpes with foil or another plate and keep them hot in the oven.

COOK'S TIP
For safety, when igniting a mixture for flambéing, use a long taper or long wooden match. Stand back as you set the mixture alight.

6 To prepare the fruit, melt the butter in a heavy frying pan, stir in the sugar and cook gently until the mixture is golden brown. Add the orange rind and juice and cook until syrupy.

7 Add the fruits and warm through, then add the liqueur and set it alight. Shake the pan to incorporate the liqueur until the flame dies down.

8 Fold the pancakes into quarters and arrange two on each plate. Spoon over some of the fruit mixture and dust liberally with the icing sugar. Serve any remaining fruit mixture separately.

BLUEBERRY PIE

AMERICAN BLUEBERRIES OR EUROPEAN BILBERRIES CAN BE USED FOR THIS PIE. YOU MAY NEED TO ADD A LITTLE MORE SUGAR IF YOU ARE LUCKY ENOUGH TO FIND WILD BILBERRIES.

SERVES SIX

INGREDIENTS
2 × 225g/8oz ready-rolled shortcrust
  pastry sheets, thawed if frozen
800g/1¾lb/7 cups blueberries
75g/3oz/6 tbsp caster (superfine)
  sugar, plus extra for sprinkling
45ml/3 tbsp cornflour (cornstarch)
grated rind and juice of ½ orange
grated rind of ½ lemon
2.5ml/½ tsp ground cinnamon
15g/½oz/1 tbsp unsalted (sweet)
  butter, diced
beaten egg, to glaze
whipped cream, to serve

1 Preheat the oven to 200°C/400°F/
Gas 6. Use one sheet of pastry to line a
23cm/9in pie pan, leaving the excess
pastry hanging over the edges.

2 Mix the blueberries, caster sugar,
cornflour, orange rind and juice, lemon
rind and cinnamon in a large bowl.
Spoon into the pastry case and dot with
the butter. Dampen the rim of the pastry
case with a little water and top with the
remaining pastry sheet.

VARIATION
Substitute a crumble topping for the
pastry lid. The contrast with the juicy
blueberry filling is sensational.

3 Cut the pastry edge at 2.5cm/1in
intervals, then fold each section over
on itself to form a triangle and create
a sunflower edge. Trim off the excess
pastry and cut out decorations from the
trimmings. Secure them to the pastry lid
with a little of the beaten egg.

4 Glaze the pastry with the egg and
sprinkle with caster sugar. Bake for
30–35 minutes or until golden. Serve
warm or cold with whipped cream.

LEMON COEUR À LA CRÈME WITH COINTREAU ORANGES

THIS ZESTY DESSERT IS THE IDEAL CHOICE TO FOLLOW A RICH MAIN COURSE SUCH AS ROAST PORK.

SERVES FOUR

INGREDIENTS
225g/8oz/1 cup cottage cheese
250g/9oz/generous 1 cup mascarpone cheese
50g/2oz/¼ cup caster (superfine) sugar
grated rind and juice of 1 lemon
spirals of orange rind, to decorate
For the Cointreau oranges
4 oranges
10ml/2 tsp cornflour (cornstarch)
15ml/1 tbsp icing (confectioners') sugar
60ml/4 tbsp Cointreau

1 Put the cottage cheese in a food processor or blender and whizz until smooth. Add the mascarpone, caster sugar, lemon rind and juice and process briefly to mix the ingredients.

2 Line four coeur à la crème moulds with muslin, then divide the mixture among them. Level the surface of each, then place the moulds on a plate to catch any liquid that drains from the cheese. Cover and chill overnight.

3 Make the Cointreau oranges. Squeeze the juice from two oranges and pour into a measuring jug (cup). Make the juice up to 250ml/8fl oz/1 cup with water, then pour into a small saucepan. Blend a little of the juice mixture with the cornflour and add to the pan with the icing sugar. Heat the sauce, stirring until thickened.

4 Using a sharp knife, peel and segment the remaining oranges. Add the segments to the pan, stir to coat, then set aside. When cool, stir in the Cointreau. Cover and chill overnight.

5 Turn the moulds out on to plates and surround with the oranges. Decorate with spirals of orange rind and serve at once.

LEMON SURPRISE PUDDING

THIS IS A MUCH-LOVED DESSERT MANY OF US REMEMBER FROM CHILDHOOD. THE SURPRISE IS THE UNEXPECTED SAUCE CONCEALED BENEATH THE DELECTABLE SPONGE.

SERVES FOUR

INGREDIENTS

   50g/2oz/¼ cup butter, plus extra
     for greasing
   grated rind and juice of 2 lemons
   115g/4oz/½ cup caster (superfine)
     sugar
   2 eggs, separated
   50g/2oz/½ cup self-raising (self-
     rising) flour
   300ml/½ pint/1¼ cups milk

1 Preheat the oven to 190°C/375°F/ Gas 5. Use a little butter to grease a 1.2 litre/2 pint/5 cup baking dish.

2 Beat the lemon rind, remaining butter and caster sugar in a bowl until pale and fluffy. Add the egg yolks and flour and beat together well. Gradually whisk in the lemon juice and milk (don't be alarmed if the mixture curdles horribly!). In a grease-free bowl whisk the egg whites until they form stiff peaks.

3 Fold the egg whites lightly into the lemon mixture, then pour into the prepared baking dish.

4 Place the dish in a roasting pan and pour in hot water to come halfway up the side of the dish. Bake for about 45 minutes until golden. Serve at once.

CRÊPES SUZETTE

SIMPLY SUPERB – THAT'S THE VERDICT ON THIS PERENNIALLY POPULAR DESSERT. THESE CRÊPES DESERVE NOTHING LESS THAN THE BEST QUALITY VANILLA ICE CREAM YOU CAN FIND.

SERVES FOUR

INGREDIENTS

   8 crêpes (see Apple Crêpes with
     Butterscotch Sauce, page 58)
   25g/1oz/2 tbsp unsalted (sweet)
     butter
   50g/2oz/¼ cup caster (superfine)
     sugar
   juice of 2 oranges
   juice of ½ lemon
   60ml/4 tbsp Cointreau or other
     orange liqueur
   best quality vanilla ice cream,
     to serve

COOK'S TIP

Crêpes freeze well and can be reheated by the method described in step 1, or simultaneously thawed and reheated in the microwave. A stack of eight crêpes, interleaved with greaseproof paper, will take 2–3 minutes on High.

1 Warm the cooked crêpes between two plates placed over a pan of simmering water.

2 Melt the butter in a heavy frying pan. Stir in the caster sugar and cook over a medium heat, tilting the pan occasionally, until the mixture is golden brown. Add the orange and lemon juices and stir until the caramel has completely dissolved.

3 Add a crêpe to the pan. Using kitchen tongs, fold it in half, then in half again. Slide to the side of the pan. Repeat with the remaining **crêpes**.

4 When all the **crêpes** have been folded in the sauce, pour over the Cointreau and set it alight. Shake the pan until the flames die down. Divide the crêpes and sauce among dessert plates and serve at once with vanilla ice cream.

CITRUS FRUIT FLAMBÉ
WITH PISTACHIO PRALINE

A FRUIT FLAMBÉ MAKES A DRAMATIC FINALE FOR A DINNER PARTY. TOPPING THIS REFRESHING CITRUS FRUIT DESSERT WITH CRUNCHY PISTACHIO PRALINE MAKES IT EXTRA SPECIAL.

SERVES FOUR

INGREDIENTS
4 oranges
2 ruby grapefruit
2 limes
50g/2oz/¼ cup butter
50g/2oz/⅓ cup light muscovado
  (brown) sugar
45ml/3 tbsp Cointreau
fresh mint sprigs, to decorate
For the praline
  oil, for greasing
  115g/4oz/½ cup caster (superfine)
    sugar
  50g/2oz/½ cup pistachio nuts

4 Heat the butter and muscovado sugar together in a heavy frying pan until the sugar has melted and the mixture is golden. Strain the citrus juices into the pan and continue to cook, stirring occasionally, until the juice has reduced and is syrupy.

5 Add the fruit segments and warm through without stirring. Pour over the Cointreau and set it alight. As soon as the flames die down, spoon the fruit flambé into serving dishes. Scatter some praline over each portion and decorate with mint. Serve at once.

1 First, make the pistachio praline. Brush a baking sheet lightly with oil. Place the caster sugar and nuts in a small heavy pan and cook gently, swirling the pan occasionally until the sugar has melted.

2 Continue to cook over a fairly low heat until the nuts start to pop and the sugar has turned a dark golden colour. Pour on to the oiled baking sheet and set aside to cool. Using a sharp knife, chop the praline into rough chunks.

3 Cut off all the rind and pith from the citrus fruit. Holding each fruit in turn over a large bowl, cut between the membranes so that the segments fall into the bowl, with any juice.

COOK'S TIP
If you like, use a rolling pin or toffee hammer to break up the praline.

COLD LEMON SOUFFLÉ <u>WITH</u> CARAMELIZED ALMOND TOPPING

THIS TERRIFIC TO LOOK AT, REFRESHING DESSERT SOUFFLÉ IS LIGHT AND LUSCIOUS.

2 Put the lemon rind and egg yolks in a bowl. Add 75g/3oz/6 tbsp of the caster sugar and whisk until light and creamy.

3 Place the lemon juice in a small heatproof bowl and sprinkle over the gelatine. Set aside for 5 minutes, then place the bowl in a pan of simmering water. Heat, stirring occasionally, until the gelatine has dissolved. Cool slightly, then stir the gelatine mixture into the egg yolk mixture.

4 In a separate bowl, lightly whip the cream to soft peaks. Fold into the egg yolk mixture and set aside.

5 Whisk the egg whites in a grease-free bowl until stiff peaks form. Gradually whisk in the remaining caster sugar until the mixture is stiff and glossy. Quickly and lightly fold the whites into the yolk mixture. Pour into the prepared dish, smooth the surface and chill for 4–5 hours or until set.

SERVES SIX

INGREDIENTS
oil, for greasing
grated rind and juice of 3 large
   lemons
5 large (US extra large) eggs,
   separated
115g/4oz/½ cup caster (superfine)
   sugar
25ml/1½ tbsp powdered gelatine
450ml/¾ pint/scant 2 cups double
   (heavy) cream
For the decoration
   75g/3oz/¾ cup flaked (sliced)
     almonds
   75g/3oz/¾ cup icing (confectioners')
     sugar
   3 physalis

1 Make the soufflé collar. Cut a strip of baking parchment long enough to fit around a 900ml/1½ pint/3¾ cup soufflé dish and wide enough to extend 7.5cm/3in above the rim. Fit the strip around the dish, tape, then tie it around the top of the dish with string. Brush the inside of the paper lightly with oil.

6 Make the decoration. Brush a baking sheet lightly with oil. Preheat the grill (broiler). Sprinkle the almonds over the sheet and sift the icing sugar over. Grill (broil) until the nuts are golden and the sugar has caramelized. Allow to cool, then remove the mixture from the tray with a metal spatula and break it into pieces.

7 When the soufflé has set, carefully peel off the parchment. Pile the caramelized almonds on top of the soufflé and decorate with the physalis.

EXOTIC FRUITS

*Who can resist the colours, textures and flavours
of delicious exotic fruits, such as mango, papaya,
passion fruit and lychee? Now that many varieties
are widely available all year, there's every excuse
for taking the taste trip and trying such delights as
Lychee and Elderflower Sorbet, Passion Fruit Crème
Caramels with Dipped Physalis, Exotic Fruit Sushi
or Melon Trio with Ginger Biscuits.*

COLD MANGO SOUFFLÉS TOPPED WITH TOASTED COCONUT

FRAGRANT, FRESH MANGO IS ONE OF THE MOST DELICIOUS EXOTIC FRUITS AROUND, WHETHER IT IS SIMPLY SERVED IN SLICES OR USED AS THE BASIS FOR AN ICE CREAM OR SOUFFLÉ.

MAKES FOUR

INGREDIENTS
4 small mangoes, peeled, stoned (pitted) and chopped
30ml/2 tbsp water
15ml/1 tbsp powdered gelatine
2 egg yolks
115g/4oz/½ cup caster (superfine) sugar
120ml/4fl oz/½ cup milk
grated rind of 1 orange
300ml/½ pint/1¼ cups double (heavy) cream
toasted flaked or coarsely shredded coconut, to decorate

COOK'S TIP
Add some juicy pieces of fresh mango on the side if you like.

1 Place a few pieces of mango in the base of each of four 150ml/¼ pint/⅔ cup ramekins. Wrap a greased collar of baking parchment around the outside of each dish, extending well above the rim. Secure with adhesive tape, then tie tightly with string.

2 Pour the water into a small heatproof bowl and sprinkle the gelatine over the surface. Leave for 5 minutes or until spongy. Place the bowl in a pan of hot water, stirring occasionally, until the gelatine has dissolved.

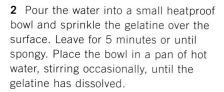

3 Meanwhile, whisk the egg yolks with the caster sugar and milk in another heatproof bowl. Place the bowl over a pan of simmering water and continue to whisk until the mixture is thick and frothy. Remove from the heat and continue whisking until the mixture cools. Whisk in the liquid gelatine.

4 Purée the remaining mango pieces in a food processor or blender, then fold the purée into the egg yolk mixture with the orange rind. Set the mixture aside until starting to thicken.

5 Whip the double cream to soft peaks. Reserve 60ml/4 tbsp and fold the rest into the mango mixture. Spoon into the ramekins until the mixture is 2.5cm/1in above the rim of each dish. Chill for 3–4 hours or until set.

6 Carefully remove the paper collars from the soufflés. Spoon a little of the reserved cream on top of each soufflé and decorate with some toasted flaked or coarsely shredded coconut.

PASSION FRUIT CRÈME CARAMELS
WITH DIPPED PHYSALIS

PASSION FRUIT HAS AN AROMATIC FLAVOUR THAT REALLY PERMEATES THESE CRÈME CARAMELS.
USE SOME OF THE CARAMEL TO DIP PHYSALIS TO CREATE A UNIQUE DECORATION.

MAKES FOUR

INGREDIENTS
- 185g/6½oz/generous ¾ cup caster (superfine) sugar
- 75ml/5 tbsp water
- 4 passion fruit
- 4 physalis
- 3 eggs plus 1 egg yolk
- 150ml/¼ pint/⅔ cup double (heavy) cream
- 150ml/¼ pint/⅔ cup creamy milk

1 Place 150g/5oz/⅔ cup of the caster sugar in a heavy pan. Add the water and heat the mixture gently until the sugar has dissolved. Increase the heat and boil until the syrup turns a dark golden colour.

2 Meanwhile, cut each passion fruit in half. Scoop out the seeds from the passion fruit into a sieve set over a bowl. Press the seeds against the sieve to extract all the juice. Spoon a few of the seeds into each of four 150ml/¼ pint/ ⅔ cup ramekins. Set the juice aside.

3 Peel back the papery casing from each physalis and dip the orange berries into the caramel. Place on a sheet of baking parchment and set aside. Pour the remaining caramel carefully into the ramekins.

4 Preheat the oven to 150°C/300°F/ Gas 2. Whisk the eggs, egg yolk and remaining sugar in a bowl. Whisk in the cream and milk, then the passion fruit juice. Strain through a sieve into each ramekin, then place the ramekins in a baking tin. Pour in hot water to come halfway up the sides of the dishes; bake for 40–45 minutes or until just set.

5 Remove the custards from the tin and leave to cool, then cover and chill for 4 hours before serving. Run a knife between the edge of each ramekin and the custard and invert each in turn on to a dessert plate, shaking the ramekins firmly to release the custards. Decorate each with a dipped physalis.

PAPAYA BAKED <u>WITH</u> GINGER

GINGER ENHANCES THE FLAVOUR OF PAPAYA IN THIS RECIPE, WHICH TAKES NO MORE THAN TEN MINUTES TO PREPARE! DON'T OVERCOOK PAPAYA OR THE FLESH WILL BECOME VERY WATERY.

SERVES FOUR

INGREDIENTS
    2 ripe papayas
    2 pieces preserved stem ginger in
      syrup, drained, plus 15ml/1 tbsp
      syrup from the jar
    8 amaretti or other dessert biscuits
      (cookies), coarsely crushed
    45ml/3 tbsp raisins
    shredded rind and juice of 1 lime
    25g/1oz/¼ cup pistachio nuts, chopped
    15ml/1 tbsp light muscovado (brown)
      sugar
    60ml/4 tbsp crème fraîche, plus extra
      to serve

VARIATION
Use Greek (US strained plain) yogurt and
almonds instead of crème fraîche and
pistachio nuts.

1 Preheat the oven to 200°C/400°F/
Gas 6. Cut the papayas in half and
scoop out their seeds. Place the halves
in a baking dish and set aside. Cut the
stem ginger into fine matchsticks.

2 Make the filling. Combine the
crushed amaretti, stem ginger
matchsticks and raisins in a bowl.

3 Stir in the lime rind and juice, two-
thirds of the nuts, then add the sugar
and the crème fraîche. Mix well.

4 Fill the papaya halves and drizzle
with the ginger syrup. Sprinkle with
the remaining nuts. Bake for about
25 minutes or until tender. Serve with
extra crème fraîche.

EXOTIC FRUIT SALAD <u>WITH</u> PASSION FRUIT DRESSING

PASSION FRUIT MAKES A SUPERB DRESSING FOR ANY FRUIT, BUT REALLY BRINGS OUT THE FLAVOUR OF EXOTIC VARIETIES. YOU CAN EASILY DOUBLE THE RECIPE, THEN SERVE THE REST FOR BREAKFAST.

<u>SERVES SIX</u>

INGREDIENTS
  1 mango
  1 papaya
  2 kiwi fruit
  coconut or vanilla ice cream, to serve
For the dressing
  3 passion fruit
  thinly pared rind and juice of 1 lime
  5ml/1 tsp hazelnut or walnut oil
  15ml/1 tbsp clear honey

COOK'S TIP
A clear golden honey scented with orange blossom or acacia blossom would be perfect for the dressing.

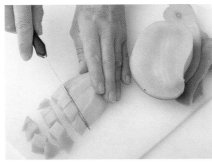

1 Peel the mango, cut it into three slices, then cut the flesh into chunks and place it in a large bowl. Peel the papaya and cut it in half. Scoop out the seeds, then chop the flesh.

2 Cut both ends off each kiwi fruit, then stand them on a board. Using a small sharp knife, cut off the skin from top to bottom. Cut each kiwi fruit in half lengthways, then cut into thick slices. Combine all the fruit in a large bowl.

3 Make the dressing. Cut each passion fruit in half and scoop the seeds out into a sieve set over a small bowl. Press the seeds well to extract all the juices. Lightly whisk the remaining dressing ingredients into the passion fruit juice, then pour the dressing over the fruit. Mix gently to combine. Leave to chill for 1 hour before serving with scoops of coconut or vanilla ice cream.

LYCHEE AND ELDERFLOWER SORBET

THE FLAVOUR OF ELDERFLOWERS IS FAMOUS FOR BRINGING OUT THE ESSENCE OF GOOSEBERRIES, BUT WHAT IS LESS WELL KNOWN IS HOW WONDERFULLY IT COMPLEMENTS LYCHEES.

SERVES FOUR

INGREDIENTS

   175g/6oz/¾ cup caster (superfine)
    sugar
   400ml/14fl oz/1⅔ cups water
   500g/1¼lb fresh lychees, peeled
    and stoned (pitted)
   15ml/1 tbsp elderflower cordial
   dessert biscuits (cookies), to serve

COOK'S TIP
Switch the freezer to the coldest setting before making the sorbet – the faster the mixture freezes, the smaller the ice crystals that form and the better the final texture will be. To ensure rapid freezing, use a metal freezerproof container and place it directly on the freezer shelf.

1 Place the caster sugar and water in a pan and heat gently until the sugar has dissolved. Increase the heat and boil for 5 minutes, then add the lychees. Lower the heat and simmer for 7 minutes. Remove from the heat and allow to cool.

2 Purée the fruit and syrup in a blender or food processor. Place a sieve (strainer) over a bowl and pour the purée into it. Press through as much of the purée as possible with a spoon.

3 Stir the elderflower cordial into the strained purée, then pour the mixture into a freezerproof container. Freeze for 2 hours, until ice crystals start to form around the edges.

4 Remove the sorbet from the freezer and process briefly in a food processor or blender to break up the crystals. Repeat this process twice more, then freeze until firm. Transfer to the fridge for 10 minutes to soften slightly before serving in scoops, with biscuits.

EXOTIC FRUIT SUSHI

THIS IDEA CAN BE ADAPTED TO INCORPORATE A WIDE VARIETY OF FRUITS, BUT TO KEEP TO THE EXOTIC THEME TAKE YOUR INSPIRATION FROM THE TROPICS. THE SUSHI NEEDS TO CHILL OVERNIGHT TO ENSURE THE RICE MIXTURE FIRMS PROPERLY, SO BE SURE YOU START THIS IN GOOD TIME.

SERVES FOUR

INGREDIENTS
150g/5oz/⅔ cup short grain
  pudding rice
350ml/12fl oz/1½ cups water
400ml/14fl oz/1⅔ cups coconut milk
75g/3oz/⅓ cup caster (superfine) sugar
a selection of exotic fruit, such as
  1 mango, 1 kiwi fruit, 2 figs and
  1 star fruit, thinly sliced
30ml/2 tbsp apricot jam, sieved
For the raspberry sauce
  225g/8oz/2 cups raspberries
  25g/1oz/¼ cup icing (confectioners')
    sugar

COOK'S TIP
To cut the rice mixture into bars, turn out of the pan, cut in half lengthways, then make 7 crossways cuts for 16 bars.

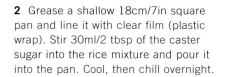

1 Rinse the rice well under cold running water, drain and place in a pan with 300ml/½ pint/1¼ cups of the water. Pour in 175ml/6fl oz/¾ cup of the coconut milk. Cook over a very low heat for 25 minutes, stirring often and gradually adding the remaining coconut milk, until the rice has absorbed all the liquid and is tender.

2 Grease a shallow 18cm/7in square pan and line it with clear film (plastic wrap). Stir 30ml/2 tbsp of the caster sugar into the rice mixture and pour it into the pan. Cool, then chill overnight.

3 Cut the rice mixture into 16 small bars, shape into ovals and flatten the tops. Place on a baking sheet lined with baking parchment. Arrange the sliced fruit on top, using one type of fruit only for each sushi.

4 Place the remaining sugar in a small pan with the remaining 50ml/4 tbsp water. Bring to the boil, then lower the heat and simmer until thick and syrupy. Stir in the jam and cool slightly.

5 To make the sauce, purée the raspberries with the icing sugar in a food processor or blender. Press through a sieve, then divide among four small bowls. Arrange a few different fruit sushi on each plate and spoon over a little of the cool apricot syrup. Serve with the raspberry sauce.

RED GRAPE AND CHEESE TARTLETS

FRUIT AND CHEESE IS A NATURAL COMBINATION IN THIS SIMPLE RECIPE. LOOK OUT FOR THE PALE, MAUVE-COLOURED OR RED GRAPES THAT TEND TO BE SLIGHTLY SMALLER THAN BLACK GRAPES. THESE ARE OFTEN SEEDLESS AND HAVE THE ADDED ADVANTAGE OF BEING SWEETER.

MAKES SIX

INGREDIENTS

    350g/12oz sweet shortcrust pastry,
      thawed if frozen
    225g/8oz/1 cup curd (farmer's) cheese
    150ml/¼ pint/⅔ cup double (heavy)
      cream
    2.5ml/½ tsp vanilla essence (extract)
    30ml/2 tbsp icing (confectioners') sugar
    200g/7oz/2 cups red grapes, halved,
      seeded if necessary
    60ml/4 tbsp apricot conserve
    15ml/1 tbsp water

VARIATIONS

Use cranberry jelly or redcurrant jelly for the glaze. There will be no need to sieve either of these. Also vary the fruit topping, if you like. Try blackberries, sliced strawberries, kiwi fruit slices, banana slices or well-drained pineapple slices.

1 Preheat the oven to 200°C/400°F/ Gas 6. Roll out the pastry and line six deep 9cm/3½in fluted individual tartlet tins (muffin pans). Prick the bases and line with baking parchment and baking beans. Bake for 10 minutes, remove the parchment and beans, then return the cases to the oven for 5 minutes until golden and fully cooked. Remove the pastry cases and cool on a wire rack.

2 Meanwhile, beat the curd cheese, double cream, vanilla essence and icing sugar in a bowl. Divide the mixture among the pastry cases. Smooth the surface and arrange the halved grapes on top.

3 Sieve the apricot conserve into a pan. Add the water and heat, stirring, until smooth. Spoon over the grapes. Cool, then chill before serving.

MELON TRIO <u>WITH</u> GINGER BISCUITS

THE EYE-CATCHING COLOURS OF THESE THREE DIFFERENT MELONS REALLY MAKE THIS DESSERT,
WHILE THE CRISP BISCUITS PROVIDE A PERFECT CONTRAST IN TEXTURE.

SERVES FOUR

INGREDIENTS
- ¼ watermelon
- ½ honeydew melon
- ½ charentais melon
- 60ml/4 tbsp stem ginger syrup

For the biscuits (cookies)
- 25g/1oz/2 tbsp unsalted (sweet) butter
- 25g/1oz/2 tbsp caster (superfine) sugar
- 5ml/1 tsp clear honey
- 25g/1oz/¼ cup plain (all-purpose) flour
- 25g/1oz/¼ cup luxury glacé (candied) mixed fruit, finely chopped
- 1 piece of preserved stem ginger in syrup, drained and chopped
- 30ml/2 tbsp flaked (sliced) almonds

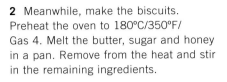

1 Remove the seeds from the melons, cut them into wedges, then slice off the rind. Cut all the flesh into chunks and mix in a bowl. Stir in the ginger syrup, cover and chill until ready to serve.

2 Meanwhile, make the biscuits. Preheat the oven to 180°C/350°F/ Gas 4. Melt the butter, sugar and honey in a pan. Remove from the heat and stir in the remaining ingredients.

3 Line a baking sheet with baking parchment. Space four spoonfuls of the mixture on the paper using half the mixture, leaving room for spreading. Flatten the mixture slightly into rounds and bake for 15 minutes or until the tops are golden.

4 Let the biscuits cool on the baking sheet for 1 minute, then lift each one in turn, using a fish slice or metal spatula, and drape over a rolling pin to cool and harden. Repeat with the remaining ginger mixture to make eight in all.

5 Serve the melon chunks with some of the syrup and the ginger biscuits.

COOK'S TIP
For an even prettier effect, scoop the melon flesh into balls with the large end of a melon baller.

BANANA AND PECAN BREAD

BANANAS AND PECAN NUTS JUST SEEM TO BELONG TOGETHER. THIS IS A REALLY MOIST AND DELICIOUS TEA BREAD. SPREAD IT WITH CREAM CHEESE OR JAM, OR SERVE AS A DESSERT WITH WHIPPED CREAM.

MAKES A 900G/2LB LOAF

INGREDIENTS

115g/4oz/½ cup butter, softened
175g/6oz/1 cup light muscovado (brown) sugar
2 large (US extra large) eggs, beaten
3 ripe bananas
75g/3oz/¾ cup pecan nuts, coarsely chopped
225g/8oz/2 cups self-raising (self-rising) flour
2.5ml/½ tsp mixed (apple pie) spice

1 Preheat the oven to 180°C/350°F/Gas 4. Grease a 900g/2lb loaf tin (pan) and line it with baking parchment. Cream the butter and sugar in a large mixing bowl until the mixture is light and fluffy. Gradually add the eggs, beating after each addition, until well combined.

2 Peel and then mash the bananas with a fork. Add them to the creamed mixture with the chopped pecan nuts. Beat until well combined.

COOK'S TIP

If the mixture shows signs of curdling when you add the eggs, stir in a little of the flour to stabilize it.

3 Sift the flour and mixed spice together and fold into the banana mixture. Spoon into the tin, level the surface and bake for 1–1¼ hours or until a skewer inserted into the centre of the loaf comes out clean. Cool for 10 minutes in the tin, then invert the tin on a wire rack. Lift off the tin, peel off the lining paper and cool completely.

DATE AND WALNUT BROWNIES

THESE RICH BROWNIES ARE GREAT FOR AFTERNOON TEA, BUT THEY ALSO MAKE A FANTASTIC DESSERT. REHEAT SLICES BRIEFLY IN THE MICROWAVE OVEN AND SERVE WITH CRÈME FRAÎCHE.

MAKES TWELVE

INGREDIENTS

350g/12oz plain (semisweet) chocolate, broken into squares
225g/8oz/1 cup butter, diced
3 large (US extra large) eggs
115g/4oz/½ cup caster (superfine) sugar
5ml/1 tsp vanilla essence (extract)
75g/3oz/¾ cup plain (all-purpose) flour, sifted
225g/8oz/1½ cups fresh dates, peeled, pitted and chopped
200g/7oz/1¾ cups walnut pieces
icing (confectioners') sugar, for dusting

COOK'S TIP

When melting the chocolate and butter, keep the water hot, but do not let it boil. Chocolate is sensitive to heat; it is vital not to let it get too hot or it may stiffen into an unmanageable mass.

1 Preheat the oven to 190°C/375°F/Gas 5. Generously grease a 30 × 20cm/12 × 8in baking tin (pan) and line with baking parchment.

2 Put the chocolate and butter in a large heatproof bowl. Place the bowl over a pan of hot water and leave until both have melted. Stir until smooth, then lift the bowl out and cool slightly.

3 In a separate bowl, beat the eggs, sugar and vanilla. Then beat into the chocolate mixture and fold in the flour, dates and nuts. Pour into the tin.

4 Bake for 30–40 minutes, until firm and the mixture comes away from the sides of the tin. Cool in the tin, then turn out, remove the paper and dust with icing sugar.